About Island Press

Since 1984, the nonprofit organization Island Press has been stimulating, shaping, and communicating ideas that are essential for solving environmental problems worldwide. With more than 1,000 titles in print and some 30 new releases each year, we are the nation's leading publisher on environmental issues. We identify innovative thinkers and emerging trends in the environmental field. We work with world-renowned experts and authors to develop cross-disciplinary solutions to environmental challenges.

Island Press designs and executes educational campaigns, in conjunction with our authors, to communicate their critical messages in print, in person, and online using the latest technologies, innovative programs, and the media. Our goal is to reach targeted audiences—scientists, policy makers, environmental advocates, urban planners, the media, and concerned citizens—with information that can be used to create the framework for long-term ecological health and human well-being.

Island Press gratefully acknowledges major support from The Bobolink Foundation, Caldera Foundation, The Curtis and Edith Munson Foundation, The Forrest C. and Frances H. Lattner Foundation, The JPB Foundation, The Kresge Foundation, The Summit Charitable Foundation, Inc., and many other generous organizations and individuals.

The opinions expressed in this book are those of the author(s) and do not necessarily reflect the views of our supporters.

Beyond Greenways

Beyond Greenways

THE NEXT STEP FOR CITY TRAILS AND WALKING ROUTES

Robert Searns

Illustrations by Bill Neumann, PLA, ASLA

ISLANDPRESS | Washington | Covelo

All rights reserved under International and Pan-American Copyright Conventions. No part of this book may be reproduced in any form or by any means without permission in writing from the publisher: Island Press, 2000 M Street, NW, Suite 480-B, Washington, DC 20036-3319.

Sketches in this book are by Bill Neumann, PLA, ASLA.

Library of Congress Control Number: 2022949364

All Island Press books are printed on environmentally responsible materials.

Manufactured in the United States of America
10 9 8 7 6 5 4 3 2 1

Keywords: 11th Street Bridge Park; 5280 Trail; accessibility; Buffalo, New York; buffering; conservation; Denver, Colorado; grand loop trail; greenway; guiding principles; hiking; Jeju Olle Trail; Maricopa Trail; master plan; mixed-use trail; pedestrian infrastructure; Phoenix, Arizona; points of access; rights of way; running; Sarasota, Florida; service nodes; Toronto, Ontario; tourism; town walk; trail depots; trail maintenance; trail management; trail running; trekking; urban shaping; Vegas Valley Rim Trail; walking; wayfinding; Wolf River Greenway

To PK and Miles

May you have as least as good an outdoors future as my outdoors past!

Contents

Prologue

*"It's a beautiful day and nature here is so delightful that I'm of a
mind to take my time . . . at a leisurely pace, rediscovering the joys
of progressing slowly, and strong bursts of endorphins soon have me
on a hiker's high."*

—Bernard Ollivier, Winds of the Steppe[1]

I've been planning and developing greenways and urban trails for five
decades. Most are paved hike/bike paths running along river and stream
corridors. I'm delighted and humbled to see their proliferation worldwide and so many people enjoying them! A few years back, contemplating the projects I'd worked on, I wondered, "What's next?" Are there
new ways to shape these kinds of spaces that offer expanded opportunities for outdoors enjoyment and ways to move more freely about on
the landscape?" While contemplating this, I had two epiphanous experiences that got me thinking about a new perspective.

The first occurred on an overnight journey to an international trails
conference on Jeju Island, South Korea. On the final segment from

Seoul to Jeju, I slipped into the bulkhead row to curl up in the window seat and get some sleep. As I squeezed past an older gentleman in the aisle seat, he nodded, and I extended a greeting. Detecting a French accent, I attempted some niceties, and we began to converse as best we could between the two languages. Bernard Ollivier was also en route to the conference. Turns out he was the keynote speaker. He had been a journalist in Paris, and he said that some time earlier, when turning sixty-two, he faced a double life crisis. Per protocol in France, he was obliged to retire, and his wife and companion of many years had recently died. On the brink, he left Paris and walked the Camino de Santiago, an ancient pilgrimage route in Spain. Inspired by that journey, he decided to embark on a much more ambitious trek: a 7,000-mile solo walk across Asia along the ancient Silk Road from Istanbul to Xi'an, China.

Bernard said his journey was incredible—a healing and consciousness-expanding experience. He has since documented his trek in a three-volume series titled *Longue Marche* (*Long Walk*). He also went on to found the Seuil Threshold Association, a healing-through-walking program offering trekking as an alternative to jail time for troubled youth offenders. Hearing that, and later reading the English translation of Bernard's epic tale, I saw walking in a new light, struck by its healing and spiritual message as well as his metaphysical way of looking at a journey on foot.

When I reached Jeju, other events and people fed into my emerging perspective, including meeting Suh Myung-sook ("Suki"). Like Bernard, Suki was a journalist, and she too, after a lengthy career, felt adrift and sought solace. She too hiked the Camino de Santiago. After her healing journey she returned with a new mission: to create the Jeju Olle, a world class trail built mostly for walking that now encircles the entire island along its edges—a 271-mile loop with the wildness of the sea on one side and towns and countryside on the other. I walked segments of this spectacular trail, and in addition to the magnificent seascapes I saw verdant rural lands, crossed stream valleys, and passed through villages, some quaint and some more developed but all interesting. I saw historic sites, heard stories about the people who lived there, and witnessed the rich culture revealed by walking the trail. I also learned about its recreational, economic, and healing benefits. Though proximate to urban areas, much of the Olle is soft surfaced, with trail treads narrower than the typical hike/bike trails found along many greenways. Although bikes are not categorically excluded, the Olle seemed more optimal for foot travel.

This new emphasis on walking I gleaned from Bernard's trek and Suki's grand loop trail stayed with me. (And by "walking" I mean foot travel in its myriad forms, including strolling, hiking, running, long-distance trekking, and even endurance training.) I left South Korea with a new perspective beyond the paved hike/bike greenway paths I'd been planning and building for decades. Also, there was something really nice about the experience of the slower pace of walking—a certain sense of freedom of not needing a bike, of just moving along step by step, no pedals, chain, or tires needed. The natural pace of walking also gave a better sense of connection—of feet to the trail, to the surrounding spaces, sounds, aromas, trees, rocks, flowers, and meeting people along the way. It was also nice to not have to be on alert for faster-moving cyclists.

In addition to the walking emphasis, the beautifully designed Jeju Olle confirmed for me the notion of a grand loop trail. It was a different kind of geometry, circular, not linear, like most greenways. Could loop trails build on the greenways notion, a significant new kind of trail infrastructure? Although I had proposed them on several plans I've written in the past, with this Jeju Olle model I felt moved to embrace the loop concept more enthusiastically. As I looked further, I saw numerous other examples. Although the Jeju Olle is one of the best, it turns out there are similar grand loops in other places, including the Maricopa

Trail around Phoenix and the Vegas Valley Rim Trail around greater Las Vegas, and Louisville, Kentucky, is building one. Interestingly, the Olmsted Brothers also planned the 40-Mile Loop for Portland over a century ago. Note that although many of these trails are hike/bike routes, I am focusing more on foot travel in this book, inspired by both Bernard and Suki.

When I returned home, the concept of the Jeju Olle stayed in my thoughts. Could we envision similar trails that run along the edges of our urban areas, where city meets countryside? They go along the edges of the wilder areas and rural places, but they are readily accessible. Like the Jeju Olle, they could offer experiences at the slower pace of walking with colorful mixes of landscapes and peoplescapes along the way. Trekking these routes could feel solitary but not isolating. You could go for an afternoon outing or do a continuous multiday trek walking on your own terms and at your own pace. Because they go through towns and village along city edges, these routes also would offer more convenient places to eat, drink, and spend the night, so no need to carry a backpack. This too is liberating. You could load essentials in a daypack and set out.

The second part of the epiphany—building shorter loop walks closer to home—came while I was working on a trail plan for Commerce City, Colorado, a working-class suburb of Denver. That project, funded largely by a local health agency, emphasized readily accessible facilities that would promote widespread routine physical activity, reducing obesity and promoting better cardiovascular fitness and overall health. In a series of neighborhood meetings two older ladies came up, and one said, "We just need places to walk, nice places, close to home." The other said, "Yeah, I just want to be able to go out my door and simply go for a walk, but the sidewalks, when they're there, are narrow and many streets are scary to cross. I just want a route, easy to get to on foot, that feels safe and pleasant!" They also expressed concern about dodging bikes on the local trails—not the first time I'd heard that concern. We seriously considered this question and recommended upgraded walking corridors with better sidewalks, safer street crossings, and other amenities such as tree medians. But the Commerce City ladies' comments lingered with me. Indeed, could we create an in-town version of the grand loops—shorter, readily accessible, pleasant walking pathways closer to people's doorsteps?

Thinking about this aspect, I decided to test the hypotheses, starting with a 6-mile walk out the front door of our apartment in a mixed-use community on the east side of Denver. I followed sidewalks and alleyways through a variety of neighborhoods, passing houses, business, parks, shops, schools, coffee places, and other elements of the urban scene. Several times, because of the lack of adequate sidewalks, I walked in the streets, the residential ones that had sparse automobile traffic. Often, I saw the locals also walking in the street, including mothers pushing strollers. I saw people, dogs, and yards, some attractively landscaped with lawns, trees, and flowers and some derelict. At no time did I feel unsafe or unwelcome except for maybe an occasional angry hound growling and gnawing on the other side of a flimsy fence. Just doing his job, I guess. Not far from home, I passed through a neighborhood of immigrants predominantly from Asia and North Africa, enjoyed the exotic dress and aromas, and discovered ethnic restaurants and grocery stores. What an experience! I never would have guessed the diversity and the sheer joy of that journey.

After that first walk, with a city map, I looked for other potential loops to sample, particularly in areas with parks, open spaces, and neighborhood shopping districts. I also realized that these loop walks could take multiple forms: tailored to communities, to employment centers, featuring civic areas and tourist destinations and ultimately offering enjoyable places to walk at every doorstep. You could even have branded loops that circle out from transit stops where anyone could ride the line, disembark at an interesting place, and walk an intriguing route.

Encouraged by the in-town walks, I decided to go big and trek around the entire edge of Greater Denver, more than 120 miles through the foothills and prairie that surround the city. I recruited a group of fellow trekkers including willing friends, family, and two dogs. I sketched out a series of 10- to 12-mile segments in Google Maps, and we met on weekends, walking one segment per outing. At the conclusion of each hike, we'd find a local restaurant, and dining with impunity because we had walked off the calories, we'd discuss our day's adventure. It was always amazing to discover the myriad rich landscapes and places on a route so close to town. We enjoyed the state parks and scenic open spaces along the way, but we also delighted in the links in between. All along the way, there were views of the mountains and expansive prairie landscapes, but you could also see the city skyline. There were intimate sights as well: barns and pastures, grazing cattle, wildlife, old plows, tractors, and even horses that came up to greet us. There were hidden streams and ponds to cool our feet and for a quick dip for the dogs, flowery meadows, old cabins, and mining artifacts, and each season had its own character and color. Occasionally, we had to make peace with an irritable canine in a yard or recalculate a route to cross a gap, but the expedition was very doable.

After we field tested the grand loop trails and in-town walk concepts, the vision of this next iteration became clearer and the potentials evident. They could be a more readily accessible alternative to more distant, harder-to-access, and increasingly crowded outdoors places like national parks and forests. Easier to reach, they could so more equitably serve diverse populations. Indeed, they can become a new kind of overlay park—places to get fit, find solace, or just get away. And in the face of increasing barriers posed by urbanization and privatization, these trails and walks would help sustain a precious right to roam so people can continue to move about freely on foot.

Trekking the edge where city meets countryside. (Credit: Robert Searns)

I also learned that walking is about more than getting from here to there; it is about being in a place, in a moment—about the joy of the journey. This book sets out to make the case that these new modes have a place, are affordable to build, and will dramatically improve the livability of our cities and the quality of our lives.

Acknowledgments

At least fifty souls helped with this book: planners, designers, engineers, advocates, health experts, and writers as well as friends, family members, and the people I met out walking. Without exception they were generous with their time, candid with their advice, and kind in sharing their thoughts, their stories, and their know-how.

I want to particularly acknowledge my wife, Sally Preston, who labored through my drafts with her pen, gave me guidance, and kept me on course. I could not have done it without her!

A special note of gratitude to Bill Neumann, PLA, ASLA, and his crew at DHM Design for preparing the illustrations that so enjoyably communicate the ideas in this book. Bill is a highly talented, creative landscape architect. Besides his project design skills, he is a top-notch illustrator and a wry cartoonist. He and I have collaborated for four decades on greenway and trail projects around the nation. I am eternally grateful to have had his skilled hand in this book!

I also thank my two editors at Island Press, Annie Byrnes and Heather Boyer, for having faith in the grand loops and town walks concept and for their invaluable wordsmithing skills and guidance. No small task!

Introduction

"We frequently walk with the sole purpose of getting from one place to another. But where are we in between? With every step we can feel the miracle of walking on solid ground. We can arrive in the present moment with every step."

—Thich Nhat Hanh[1]

If I were to use a single word to express the current times, the stress, the pressure, the constant barrage of "breaking news," pending doom and gloom from pandemics to climate change, I would say "confined." Maybe "trapped" is a better word. Sedentary behavior and screen time increased during the COVID-19 pandemic. According to the US National Institute of Health, 51 percent of adults and 67 percent of children reported increases in total screen time, and 52 percent of adults and 60 percent of children reported increases in leisure screen time.[2] Although for many the illusion of a "get-away" is there, we need more.

According to the US Centers for Disease Control and Prevention (CDC), more than 42 percent of the people in the United States are obese and are increasingly suffering from the associated health impacts, including diabetes and cardiovascular disease. And although this problem is widespread across all peoples, minority communities and lower-income populations are particularly prone with rates at least 14 percent higher.[3] Given that very troubling health concern, it's not surprising that the CDC specifically cites the need for "safe, convenient, places to walk . . . places to move about . . . protected from traffic and safe from crime and hazards." Routine walking has myriad health benefits, including preventing and managing health conditions such as heart disease and type 2 diabetes, increasing energy levels, and strengthening the immune system.[4] Sometimes you must go out the door, just walk, nothing programmed or highly structured, be in nature, and walk pleasurably without trepidation or conflict.

Getting out on trails and walking routes was one of the few ways to break the confinement of COVID lockdowns. The Outdoor Industry Association reported that in the United States, what they refer to as "day hiking" increased by over 8 percent during the first year of the pandemic.[5] With a reasonable modicum of safety and comfort, you could get outdoors, enjoy nature, and to some extent socialize. For many this was a godsend, and for planners it was a lesson learned. Walking is a simple activity that practically anyone can do. The challenge for many is finding those places and being able to access them easily. Although we have existing parks, greenways, and urban trails, in these times those are not enough—people need more places to walk.

Tied to this is the need to have more places to freely enjoy the outdoors, especially rights of way for walking on the land. A right to roam addresses a core human need. Although in many places throughout the world there is a welcoming view of roaming in the outdoors, attitudes toward this kind of travel and connectivity in the United States increasingly lean toward exclusion. There is distrust and downright fear of outsiders, even disdain for the public, especially on or even near one's property. Yet there is simultaneously an exploding demand for trails and outdoor places. Overcrowding and overuse of both existing urban trails and more remote backcountry places such as national forests, national parks, and state parks is a growing problem. Add climate change to the mix along with concerns about wildfires, invasive species, and infestations like the bark beetle, and it gets even worse. No doubt, more restrictions and even access rationing is coming—no more spontaneous visits but access by reservation only, if at all. There is also the question of equitable access to these places by diverse populations. These growing limitations tie, in a significantly worsening way, to the sense of confinement and feeling trapped.

And many of us live in places where its unsafe or unpleasant just to take a walk from the front door. If I were to use a single word to describe the challenge to walkability, it would be "disconnected." Although there are multiple factors that fragment our spaces, none is as profound as the impact of the automobile. Our contemporary landscape is the result of more than a century of expanding automobile infrastructure. Motor vehicles create noise and fumes including dangerous levels of air pollution, and they are a major cause of serious pedestrian injuries and deaths—according to the CDC, over 104,000 injuries and over 7,000 fatalities in the United States annually.[6] There is also the very deleterious impact of barriers to foot travel created by highways and arterial streets as well as inadequate and unpleasant walking environments. In addition to the barriers created by the freeways and arterials, there are other impediments such as cul-de-sacs and poor sidewalks, or none at all, in many residential and commercial areas. Figure 0.1 illustrates a daunting intersection.

We not only need more places to walk, but we also need more people to want to use them. Walking, running, and hiking are the first, second, and third most popular activities in the United States, with more than 145 million people (6 in 10) participating. That's the good news. The

Figure 0.1. Difficult intersections pose barriers to safe and pleasant travel. (Credit: Robert Searns)

challenge is that there are tens of millions who don't participate, with dire health and wellbeing consequences.[7]

The Next Generation of Urban Trails

Although greenways and backcountry trails have helped address these needs, we need more trails, and we need more of those trails to be accessible and inviting to a greater percentage of the population in the United States. In this book I suggest a new generation of trails, which fall into two categories: grand loop trails and town walks.

Grand loop trails are longer-distance routes that encircle cities running along the parameters where city meets countryside. In effect, grand loop trails are a closer-in alternative to backcountry routes. They could be from 20 miles to 300 miles or more in length, laid out around cities along the urban–rural edge to offer a backcountry-like or bucolic experience. Being closer in, they are more reachable than more remote hiking trails by a shorter car trip, local transit, or a rideshare service. One could take an afternoon hike or plan a multiday trek.

Town walks are 2- to 6-mile loops built in neighborhoods, downtowns, or other urban and suburban places. Depending on where they are located and how they are laid out, town walks have a range of functions. Some may be tourist-oriented draws that showcase a city's special civic spaces and iconic attractions. Others would serve more localized needs such as neighborhood walking routes that could be easily enjoyed after work or on a lunch hour. These would promote routine enjoyment and exercise. They can also serve as practical routes to walking distance destinations, although the primary purpose is recreation and fitness. Ideally, one day, they will be convenient to every doorstep. Eventually these loops, along with greenways and other trails, could form metrowide, green overlay networks that enhance urban landscapes.

In a number of places, this exciting new generation of trails and walking routes is already being built. In 2004, the Maricopa County Board of Supervisors approved a plan for the Maricopa Trail,[8] a 315-mile trail along the edges of greater Phoenix, Arizona, linking county parks and other treasured landscapes together. Around the same time, Suh Myungsook, a journalist looking for a new direction, envisioned the Jeju Olle,[9] an incredible 271-mile pathway—a grand loop—that would completely encircle Jeju, a Maui-like island off the coast of South Korea. The Phoenix and Jeju trails are both now built, and there are similar metro-edge trails in the works that will encircle Las Vegas, Nevada,[10] Louisville, Kentucky,[11] and Denver, Colorado.[12] Toronto, Ontario,[13] also has a trail program in place that envisions a spectacular grand loop. Interestingly, Toronto's city edge project goes hand in hand with a robust greenbelt system where one promotes the other.

In 2006, Gayle Hartman and Marjorie Cunningham, both history buffs, envisioned a 2½-mile walking loop around Tucson's historic district that would connect and reveal its iconic civic buildings, the old barrios, ethnic restaurants, and other places. They took the idea to the Presidio Museum Trust, procured some leftover paint from the city, and laid out the Turquoise Trail.[14] Today, thousands visit, including history buffs, tourists, and locals just wanting to enjoy a pleasant, informative walk. It's the best way to experience the "authentic" Tucson! Like the Turquoise Trail, there are several other notable similar projects. Ashville, North Carolina, boasts its 1.7-mile Urban Trail,[15] with sculptures and historic sites, and in 2021, Denver voters approved a bond initiative kicking off development of the 5280 Trail,[16] a world-class 5-mile loop around the edges of that city's downtown area.

These projects represent how greenways—along with other urban trails and walking routes—can evolve to offer more opportunities to recreate and to make these places more readily accessible. They suggest the potential for an intriguing new iteration beyond the typical linear greenway that follows established corridors such as rivers or repurposed rail routes. Instead, these are loops, not confined to preexisting corridors as many greenways are. The pathways envisioned in this book embrace characteristics of greenways but go a step further to include walkable streetscapes in the city and comfortable hiking path loops running through fields and forests on the edges of cities.

In building on the greenway concept, there are four important differences when considering grand loops and town walks: They have a different geometry, they are more adaptable and easier to build, they are more accessible, and as presented here, there is an emphasis on walking.

Starting with geometry, they represent a new green overlay shape that goes from linear to loop. Whereas traditional greenways typically follow existing corridors in the landscape such as rivers, streams, and old railroad track routes, grand loops and town walks cut across the grain of the terrain. The potential trail corridors expand from being down by the river or along a rail line to more ubiquitous routes. In effect the entire metroscape becomes the canvas on which we can lay them out. They can reach more places and be accessed by more people and thus offer more equitably and widely available outdoor experiences. They also provide alternative outdoor destinations to increasingly crowded and remote places such as national forests and national parks.

There is more flexibility in the ways they can be built because they are envisioned primarily as walking routes—not the typical engineered, paved hike and bike paths built along greenways. This means more adaptability. Properly planned and designed, not only can they follow what we typically think of as trail routes, but, where conditions are right, they can be overlaid on existing infrastructure including low-traffic roads, local streets, and sidewalks. Not having to accommodate bikes—at least not road bikes—these trails are much simpler and less costly to build and maintain. They can even be established at the rudimentary level with just some signs or paint on the sidewalk, like the Turquoise Trail in Tucson.

The emphasis on walking—as opposed to bicycling—might be a little controversial for some but, based on my experiences of successful walking-oriented routes such as the Jeju Olle, where on-foot travel is so popular, and from the input of many public meetings where participants repeatedly asked for tranquil places to walk where they didn't have to frequently jump out of the way of faster-moving bikes, I saw the need for a travel-on-foot emphasis. (Note that for purposes of this book, the term "walking" includes its myriad variations—hiking, running, wheelchair travel, and, in places, even horseback riding.) Does this mean you can't visualize grand loops and town walks as bike paths? Of course not! Certainly, almost any of the types of paths proposed in this book could be designed to accommodate bicycles, especially mountain bikes, that don't require pavement, if the advocates so wish. And several of the projects mentioned as examples in this book, including the loops around Las Vegas and Louisville, have shared-use hike/bike paths. So designing them for biking is always an option.

This book introduces these routes as a next step for envisioning close-in, readily accessible green places to recreate. It builds on the successes of the greenway movement as a new breed of high-quality, readily accessible outdoor spaces in and around cities. The chapters that follow further define these routes and provide guidance on how to plan, design, and implement them. We will see how they can be a new kind of park that can be integrated into, and shape, city landscapes, strengthening connectivity and helping to preserve and create high-quality public places. We'll also see how they can offer more widely and equitably accessible routes to roam, giving more people the opportunity to enjoy the act of moving through the outdoors under their own power. Grand loops and town walks not only offer close-in ways to enjoy the outdoors, but they can create a layer of affordable green infrastructure. They can welcome and enable a broader and more culturally diverse cross-section of peoples and promote health and fitness. The concepts laid out here envision a new kind of pathway tailored for twenty-first-century needs and conditions. Like the traditional hierarchy of parks—regional, community, and neighborhood parks—grand loops and town walks have levels that define them. A grand loop that completely encircles metro areas can be seen as a regional park. A town walk can be seen as a kind of neighborhood, community, or even a citywide park overlay.

Along with emphasizing the joys and benefits of walking as a mode of outdoor engagement, there is an emphasis on traveling with just a daypack. A walker could go on a multiday trip on a grand loop trail, traveling light, around the edges of the city. Someone on a day outing could easily find places to dine and get provisions. On longer trek, a hiker could stay at an inn, campground. or other close-in lodging.

When we look at more recent trends in the ways that traditional parks are built and used, we see other opportunities for grand loops and town walks as places to exercise and find solace. Many traditional parks have increasingly become places for organized sports, with playfields, basketball, and tennis courts. As one scholarly paper puts it, "A city park no longer works in the same ways it did in the nineteenth and twentieth centuries. It is (now) rarely a place for . . . experiencing a pastoral contrast to the dense city or contemplating nature—the purposes for which it was originally intended."[17] The authors go on to say that "a vital neighborhood needs to no longer maintain an area isolated as a 'park' in proportion to population. Rather, it should be one that brings green pathways through the streets."[18] Grand loops and town walks could fit this alternative model better, meeting a range of contemporary needs.

This book also has an implicit message about resilience. Increasingly, when experts and advocates talk about addressing the profound problems of the day, such as climate change and other formidable issues, they talk about resilience. Grand loops and town walks are not all-encompassing solutions, but they have a place. Ideally, by providing closer-in, safe, and accessible walking paths we can offer green places in and around the edges of town, which will lead to less automobile-oriented travel to more distant places as people seek refuge from cities. There are also opportunities to set aside special conservation areas along trails. The Appalachian Trail epitomizes this with a spin-off of the Appalachian Conservation Trust that, through its landscape conservation initiatives, has protected tens of thousands of acres along the trail route.[19] Another environmental organization, Ecosystem Restoration Camps, is already doing this with more than forty such places where visitors work on reforestation and other landscape rehabilitation projects, on six continents. There is an opportunity to have these as a regular feature of grand loop trails.[20]

This book aims to build on the legacy of parks, parkways, greenways, and urban trails by offering a consistent, practical guide to promoting and implementing them as new outdoor opportunities and solutions to number of contemporary challenges. The goals are also to serve and motivate practitioners and academicians; open space, city planning, and park agencies; and civic and business leaders, conveying the notion that building high-quality walking corridors and urban edge trails can bring myriad benefits and reach "everyday people," not only outdoors and fitness enthusiasts but also those who are looking for ways to be more active, both at home and when traveling.

In beginning to formulate the ideas in this book, I wondered whether communities and officials would want to invest in them. At first there was some trepidation because it was something new, maybe just crazy. Then I began to see news articles about the Phoenix, Las Vegas, and Louisville projects and learned about the Turquoise and 5280 trails. In the Phoenix case, Maricopa County committed $5 million up front to build that grand loop. In Denver, the loop will be a $100 million effort with a profound reshaping and beautification of the streetscapes along the 5-mile route. It turns out that voters okayed millions in startup dollars. People are not only thinking about these new kinds of trails but also approving the funds to build them. Some places are building grand loops and town walks, but promoting more of them requires not only introducing the idea but making the case. Here are some key talking points:

They meet a fundamental human need. Walking is in our genes. It is a pillar of what makes us human, the most primitive and the longest-enduring mode of human travel, the ability—and necessity—to move about, under our own power. It is an essential need for all of us, a universal aspect in our daily lives that permeates nearly all cultures. We can look at trails and pathways not only as routes of travel but also as transcendent places.

They offer more and safer walkability. In an era dominated by the automobile and barriers that automobile infrastructure imposes, they can offer a counterpoint: enjoyable, safe places to walk. Though not the total answer, with better sidewalks and safer street crossings, they can help reduce the staggering toll of pedestrian accidents.

They can be an alternative to more crowded outdoor destinations. With more crowding and difficulty of accessing outdoor places, they offer a closer-in, more widely and equitably accessible recreational alternative.

They bring health and wellbeing benefits. With increasing problems of obesity and other serious health problems including mental health problems and stress, they can promote fitness—and solace—by enabling and encouraging more frequent walking and moving about in the outdoors.

They promote a better environment. They can promote better environmental stewardship and address urban sprawl by defining green spaces along the city edges and revitalizing neighborhoods by creating attractive places to walk in town. They address climate change, reducing emissions by promoting less driving with closer-in places to recreate. Motor vehicles account for nearly a third of carbon emissions.[21]

Increasingly the notion of resilience fits into this discussion. Taking practical, doable interim steps to adapt and adjust pending more encompassing solutions to massive problems such as climate change promotes resilience.

They bring economic benefits. They promote economic development by encouraging people to patronize restaurants, convenience stores, coffee shops, lodging, and other support services and by improving the character and property value of neighborhoods with new park-like overlays.

They help ensure a future with places to roam. They will establish and preserve walking routes and connectivity in the face of increasing urban sprawl, more barriers, and overcrowded outdoor destinations.

They are places for people who just want to have fun. They are simply a fun thing to do—a new mode of leisure activity at home and when traveling.

The book sets out to introduce a new concept and ways to realize results. It has three parts. The first section defines grand loops and town walks and makes the case for building them. Next comes practical advice on how to plan and design them and how to secure rights of way. The third part lays out how to go from vision to reality, to garner support, assemble resources, get them built, and motivate people to use them. This section wraps up with a series of thought experiments where the grand loops and town walks are conceptually tested out in several different cities across a range of climate conditions, terrains, and cultural values.

Please note that this is not a technical trail design manual. There are already many excellent resources, some of which are referenced at the end of the book, that already do this. Rather, this is a guide to envisioning, laying out, and promoting these routes and, in so doing, realizing the benefits they offer—to facilitate, encourage, and enable more close-in walking, hiking, running, and trekking and to significantly improve the quality of the places where we live and visit by creating these routes. Because this is a somewhat novel concept that is still evolving, each reader is encouraged to use the ideas and guidance in the chapters. It is a starting place you can build on, adding in your own approaches to planning and design. At the end of the day, the goal is about offering readily accessible, high-quality trails and walking places to anyone who wants to enjoy them, motivating and enabling more people to engage in this kind of outdoor activity, and improving our cities with a new layer of parklike green infrastructure so that, one day, every doorstep is a trailhead.

CHAPTER 1

The Next Step for City Trails and Walking Routes

*"As rights of way determined and sustained by use,
they constitute a labyrinth of liberty."*

—Robert Macfarlane, *The Old Ways*[1]

Recently, our daughter set out on a weekend backpacking trip to a national forest outside Denver, Colorado, that used to be an hour away. Later that same day, she and her husband, and their dog, showed up at our door. I asked her what happened, and she said, "Dad, we turned back, it was bumper to bumper, and we didn't know if we could find a place to camp or even a place to park at a trailhead." They just wanted to get away, out of the city, to enjoy some green space and hike a trail. Colorado, where we live, was once the backyard of the nation. Now, with the state's population headed toward 6 million, one faces a gauntlet of traffic, permit requirements, and crowds. There are impediments not only to accessing the backcountry but also to accessing local outdoor destinations.

Compounding this problem is the further privatization of the commons. One particularly disturbing example is the growing trend of "amenity ranches" where the rich buy up open lands either individually or as a group to ensure that they will have a place to hike, hunt, fish, or just enjoy being in nature. Increasingly, developers are buying large tracts of open land, particularly along rivers or other scenic places. They then sell off lots to buyers, who put up houses. Many times, they put up fences and no trespassing signs, giving the message that the public is not welcome. According to a 2022 *New York Times* article, rising numbers of ranches purchased as country escapes have "brought new attitudes toward strangers pursuing activities like hiking . . . on land that may have previously been public or treated as such."[2]

Ken Ilgunas, a journalist and author of the book *Trespassing Across America*, writes that "even where there aren't signs, Americans know they don't have the implicit permission to visit their town's neighboring woods, fields, and coastlines. Long gone are the days when we could." He raises the question of who has the right to roam, to move freely about the landscape, safely and pleasantly on foot along high-quality routes of travel. Ilgunas adds that we need to reconsider what he calls the "right to exclude." In many ways its seems that unless you drive a car, pay a fee, or have a reservation, you don't have the ability to enjoy the outdoors easily and spontaneously.[3] This sense of exclusion is further compounded when we consider people who don't fit the accepted racial, ethnic, or gender profiles. As a Trust for Public Lands study puts it, more than 100 million Americans "don't have a park close to home and are vying for the same patch of outdoor space as many of [their] neighbors . . . [and] too often this is the case for low-income neighborhoods and communities of color." The study suggests that a solution would be to "energize and accelerate the efforts of historically marginalized communities" in order to help close the park equity gap.[4]

The Sierra Club in its Outdoors for All program also highlights this concern, recommending not curtailing access to outdoor space but rather increasing it by conserving more land and removing barriers to entry from those who feel excluded or unable to access the outdoors.[5]

Over recent decades there have been trends and movements to establish trails and other outdoor corridors, particularly greenways, as places to recreate in and near cities. This trend has helped, but alone it has not been enough. There is a need for a more comprehensive approach to outdoor places that are more easily and spontaneously accessible.

Since the times when people first left the countryside to settle in cities, there has been a desire for green urban infrastructure, for places of refuge from the harsher aspects of city life. Indeed, creating and setting aside pleasurable green spaces accessible to urban dwellers is a centuries-old form of landscape adaptation.[6] Parks, commons, civic squares, tree-lined boulevards, and parkways have long been a counterpoint to the loss of access to natural landscapes and the solace these places have provided. These green spaces, carved out in cities, have helped mitigate crowded living conditions, oppressive factories, and other bleak conditions urban dwellers face. More recently, greenways have evolved from the more traditional parks and parkways as places of respite. In the case of greenways, they were also a response to automobile-dominated living conditions. On a greenway you escape from the noise of traffic and a enjoy a quieter tree-lined trail. Greenway planners have also strived to preserve and restore valued natural corridors such as rivers and streams.

Inspired by the greenway concept, grand loops and town walks go a step further in alleviating the ills of urbanization as a new iteration of adaptive green infrastructure. They evolve from the legacy of boulevards, parks, parkways, and greenways. To understand how grand loops and town walks fit into this process, let's take a closer look at that legacy.

The Evolution of Adaptive Green Infrastructure

We consider three generations of parklike corridors that form the foundation of the grand loop trails and town walks concept: the ancestral axes and boulevards, parkways, and greenways. These three predecessors, along with grand loops and town walks, share the commonality that they offer routes of travel, not so much for getting from point A to point B, but for recreation, solace, and enjoyment.

The First Generation: Axes and Boulevards

To start, we look back over 3,000 years, to China, to find these ancestral routes. Sometimes called axes, these were attractive, specially defined corridors, typically connecting important buildings, markets, and other places in cities. They were for gathering and daily travel and were often celebratory elements of civic life for special events and processions. They were a counterpoint to the drudgery of daily life and crowded living conditions. Often, they were integrated into networks. According to noted landscape architect John Ormsbee Simonds, axes were "directional, orderly and dominating" routes of travel.[7] They became unifying and city-shaping landscape elements.

Over the subsequent millennia, axes evolved into boulevards, the most famous prototypes appearing in the seventeenth century at the Versailles Palace of Louis XIV. And, of course, the Champs-Élysées of Paris is a prototypical boulevard. These routes were majestic, tree lined, and deliberately laid out not only to connect and celebrate important places but also to provide a spectacular civic space experience both for grand events and for those just strolling these routes daily. While they served royalty and other high officials, they were also intended as places for the people—impressive, public garden spaces.

This "grand avenues" concept was adopted by urban planners such as Pierre Charles L'Enfant, who laid out Washington, DC, and they became the unifying elements of many of the world's great cities from Paris to Buenos Aires. Even Las Vegas has its unifying celebratory axis, the Strip, although that route could use more shade. Many are, or were, for walking. In more current times, automobiles have claimed the dominant portion of many of these spaces.

The Second Generation: Parkways

In the late nineteenth century, Frederick Law Olmsted, considered the father of landscape architecture, inspired in part by the boulevards, went one step further and envisioned parkways. Beginning in pre-automobile times, Olmsted's parkways were a new kind of roadway for both carriages and pedestrians. He saw them as "picturesque in character" and "bordered by a small belt of trees and shrubbery."[8] In so doing, he combined the functions of movement, use, views, and experience with a goal of introducing nature back into the city. These corridors focused on linking parks and other green spaces rather than palaces, government buildings, or granite edifices. Obsessed with health, wellbeing, and spiritual solace, Olmsted sought to create readily accessible outdoor places of refuge and recovery as a counterpoint to the oppressive factories and bleak industrial settings.

In 1866, after the war as he finished the Central Park Plan for New York, he proposed a parkway for Brooklyn. The main feature was a 55-foot-wide, central roadway that also served as a pleasure drive. Traffic was reserved for carriages and other light vehicles. On either side of the road were 35-foot-wide "malls" where residents could play, stroll, and relax. This is what became Eastern Parkway.[9] Along with his partner, Calvert Vaux, they saw this as the catalyst of what could become a vast chain of parks and landscaped pleasure drives, forming a continuous leafy route, or a "shaded green ribbon," running throughout

the New York metropolitan area. Civic leaders saw these routes as outdoor places of refuge from "noxious or offensive" businesses, including
slaughterhouses, foundries, and glue factories. "With the wide planting
area afforded in the parkways . . . and robust trees, these 'boulevards,'"
according to road historian Dan Marriott, would be places with "thriving, large canopies growing to their true and beautiful form . . . a green
space, with mature trees, nice shadow patterns, cooling breezes, rustling
leaves, and shady walks less of a street and more of a park, hence the
term 'parkway.'"[10]

Today the Eastern Parkway runs for several miles through central
Brooklyn from Prospect Park almost to Highland Park, featuring pedestrian and bike lanes and about twenty-five species of trees.[11] Olmsted
and Vaux soon moved on to other places, including the industrial city
of Buffalo, New York. In the 1870s, they planned what many consider
to be the nation's first linear park system, where parks were expressed as
green corridors rather than as a single area. Indeed, building that unifying network of beautiful park nodes and parkways defined the character
of, and linked together, many of Buffalo's residential districts. Much of
the system is still in place today, although parts of it now lay under a
freeway. Similar plans were drawn up for Boston, Chicago, Louisville,
and other North American cities.[12]

The Third Generation: Greenways

In the late 1960s, the next iteration of the linear green corridors
emerged: greenways. By the mid-twentieth century, the automobile had
become the new "industrial age nemesis." Now, instead of bleak industrial landscapes of Olmsted's time, cars, trucks, and buses took over
almost "total domination of North American cityscapes."[13] They were
noisy, smelly, and hazardous, not only to the people in the vehicles but
also to folks on foot. Busy roadways, especially arterials and freeways,

become formidable barriers. Urban advocates and planners looked for alternatives to the auto-dominated roadways. According to Charles Little, urbanist William Holly Whyte probably first coined the word *greenway* in a 1959 monograph titled *Securing Open Space for America*, although Little also credits urban planner Edmund Bacon with early use of the term when he proposed a greenway network for a development northwest of Philadelphia. Whyte further defined greenways in the late 1960s when he wrote, "There are all sorts of opportunities to link separated spaces together," and "ingenuity can accomplish a great deal. Our metropolitan areas are crisscrossed with connective strips. Many are no longer in use. But they are there if we only look."[14,15]

A decade later, in the early 1970s, some US cities began to envision greenways as a new iteration of parkways. Whereas parkways primarily followed street and automobile corridors, greenways were seen as pedestrian- and bicycle-oriented routes designed to run primarily along natural systems such as rivers or steams, although some also followed canals and rail routes.

In 1974, Denver was one of the first places to adapt greenways as urban green corridors. Raleigh, North Carolina, also initiated a greenway program that same year. In Denver civic leaders proposed a 10-mile linear park along the length of the long-abused South Platte River through the heart of the city. Planners there adopted the name *greenway*, and it stuck. Coincidentally, Raleigh embraced the same moniker. Like Olmsted's parkways, the Platte River Greenway linked parks, plazas, and other features, with an 8-foot-wide warm tone concrete hike/bike path being single unifying element—besides the river itself. By the early 1980s, the Platte River Greenway ran the length of the city. And following that, the greenway system expanded along the river and its tributaries into the wider metro region. In less than two decades, greater Denver had a trail and greenway network extending for hundreds of miles. Raleigh's system similarly grew. Over the subsequent decades, the greenway idea spread and took hold with projects in cities across North America and worldwide.[16]

In *Greenways for America*, Charles Little describes the burgeoning greenway phenomenon as it was emerging in the 1980s and 1990s. This movement brought forth a whole new genre of trails, particularly urban trails. In his definitions, Little emphasizes their linear character as mostly following ingrained corridors such as rivers, railroads, and sometimes a ridgeline. Most greenways have been built for bicycling as well as walking.

Little defines a greenway as 1. "A linear open space established along either a narrow corridor, such as a riverfront, stream valley, or ridgeline, or overland along a railroad right-of-way converted to recreational use, a canal, a scenic road, or other route. 2. Any natural or landscaped course for pedestrian or bicycle passage. 3. An open space connector linking parks, nature reserves, cultural facilities, or historic sites with each other and populated areas. 4. Locally, certain strip or linear parks designated as a parkway or greenbelt."[17]

The *greenway* moniker expanded to include concepts of larger, interconnected metropolitan-wide trail and greenway networks and even mega greenways, which span nations. This larger vision, inspired in part by earlier long-distance routes such as the Appalachian Trail, led to a number of projects including the East Coast Greenway, which runs between Key West, Florida and Calais, Maine, and a Czech Greenway that connects Prague to Vienna. Though not labeled a greenway, the 15,000-mile coast-to-coast Trans Canada Trail extends from St. Johns, Newfoundland, to Victoria, British Columbia. The original greenway concept further evolved to incorporate riparian restoration, better floodplain management, wildlife connectivity corridors, and places for ecological interpretation and education as well as historical and cultural preservation.

Since their introduction, greenways have been enhancing communities and the ways people recreate worldwide. Today, greenways are a worldwide movement, and they're found practically everywhere, reshaping cities and expanding the ways people recreate. They've been a wonderful addition, with trails and naturalistic corridors, to our recreational and environmental infrastructure. However, after nearly five decades of planning and developing greenways, I began to wonder whether they were enough. In both my professional and personal outdoor life, I noticed unsolved challenges such as lack of easy access to facilities, overcrowding, and conflicts between users. I asked myself, What could be the next step?

Grand Loops and Town Walks: The Next Step

With this context of adaptive green places in mind, we look to grand loop trails and town walks, the next step beyond greenways. Like their predecessors, boulevards, parkways, and greenways, grand loops and town walks offer a new layer and mode of green infrastructure that is also an adaptive counterbalance to the urban living adversities and impediments of the times. In an era of more crowded open spaces and impeded mobility, they can lessen the difficulty of accessing outdoor places.

Greenways are generally linear. The grand loops and town walks have a new geometry, primarily loops. Rather than following geological features dictated by the terrain, loops typically cut across the grain of the urbanscape. In so doing, loops are not confined to established corridors such as rivers or rail routes. By being more flexible, they can connect more places and landscapes together and reach more people. Loops can also link linear trail elements such as greenways together. In fact, the greenways can serve as spokes connecting neighborhoods and city centers to loops, enabling broader, more diverse access by urban dwellers.

Let's start here with an overall definition of grand loop trails and town walks.

Grand loop trails encircle cities along the edges where city meets countryside.

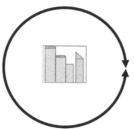

Town walks are shorter loop pathways located in cities. There are three subcategories of town walks, and their characteristics depend on their locations and planning objectives:

• *Destination walks*: routes that highlight, connect, or feature civic spaces, tourist destinations, and other major urban attractions.

• *Community walks*: branded, high-quality walking loops readily accessible from neighborhoods and places of employment.

• *Doorstep walks*: readily and spontaneously accessible walking routes at each doorstep. These aren't defined routes. Rather, each person finds their own way. Establishing these routes involves promoting policies that lead to widespread, ultimately ubiquitous urban walking infrastructure.

Together, these route types form a palette of options to choose from in creating exciting new systems of trails and walking amenities. They can also interconnect, form networks, and complement each other. We could also view these as a new form of overlay parks, giving people a range of choices. The surfaces can vary from dirt to gravel, to paved paths and sidewalks. We also can include country lanes and any street where traffic volumes and speeds are low enough to provide a safe, pleasant walking experience. In some instances, they might even be delineated by painted pedestrian lane markings, the walking version of a bike lane. The variety of potential surfaces adds flexibility to building these trails, often at a lower cost than paved hike/bike pathways.

This book emphasizes walking. However, we don't want to exclude bikes and other mechanical devices, such as scooters, from the planning process. In many instances project advocates will want a multiuse trail. This was certainly the case with the Las Vegas Valley Rim Trail, the Louisville Loop Trail, and the Denver 5280 Trail. In some instances, primarily in the case of town walks, plans include paved surfaces for road bikes. In other cases, such as the Maricopa Trail around Phoenix, mountain biking is popular. The path is not paved but has a dirt surface that accommodates these types of bikes. Increasingly, electric powered e-bikes will come into the picture on both grand loop and town walk projects.

Where bikes or other nonmotorized mechanical devices are a necessary part of the picture, the goal is to facilitate a safe, enjoyable experience for all participants and to minimize conflicts. An important element of this is the notion of flow. The term, coined by psychologist Mihaly Csikszentmihalyi, describes a state where flow is "a state in which people are so involved in an activity that nothing else seems to matter; the experience is so enjoyable that people will continue . . . for the sheer sake of doing it."[18]

Ideally, a person walking does not want to have to be vigilant for bikes, and most bikers probably do not want to have to stop the flow of their ride experience to brake for slow-moving walkers. Although most polite bikers and hikers accommodate each other, typically there is a visceral difference in the ways that riders and walkers want to enjoy their experiences. Trail expert Tony Boone suggests that riding is a kinesthetic awareness activity, whereas walking and hiking are aesthetic awareness activities. Not placing a value judgement, Tony says, "There are different sensory parts engaged." "Kinesthetic is more in your joints and ear canals. The aesthetic is more in the 'the heart and soul.'" It's about the "rush versus the wildflowers," as he puts it.[19]

In wrapping up the thoughts here about bikes, it is useful to note that whereas the Las Vegas and Louisville examples suggest a paved multiuse (hike/bike) trail surface, Phoenix's Maricopa Trail was built as primarily four-wide "earthen surface not designed for street bikes," as parks agency director RJ Cardin puts it. He adds, though, that "it is suitable for mountain and hybrid bikes and there is often that kind of use."[20] Although the emphasis is still on walking, bikes will undoubtedly enter the picture, so it's important to be ready to thoughtfully address this potential use.

There are no simple answers when planning and designing for mixed use. It's probably best done on a case-by-case basis. For each user group's needs and preferences to work, the key is to minimize conflicts between mechanized and nonmechanized recreationalists. This might mean shared-use, dual trails with foot and bike travel on separate treads or side loops designed for bikes. Designing for shared uses is addressed further in Chapter 5.

Having laid out the basic concepts, let's now look at the characteristics of each type in more detail. Note that the subsequent chapters will go into greater depth regarding different characteristics, themes, layouts, design, and specific alignments of grand loops and town walks.

Grand Loop Trails

Built on the outskirts of town in the woods, hills, and fields, these are more appropriately called trails. Ideally, they have an earthen or crushed gravel surface wide enough for two people to walk side by side (4–6 feet), although this is not always the case. Depending on conditions and resources, the trail width and surface will probably vary, and in places the trail may even follow low-traffic backroads and country lanes. They are carefully planned to run through attractive settings, emphasizing vistas and having vegetated buffered edges to create a backcountry feel whenever possible. In many instances a grand loop trail will link larger city edge open spaces such as regional preserves or state parks.

Portland Oregon's 40-Mile Loop is the granddaddy of grand loops. First proposed in 1904 by the Olmsted brothers, it was seen as an interconnected system of "scenic reservations and parkways." Although it was initially slow in its implementation, advocates, led by the 40-Mile Loop Land Trust, picked up the idea in the 1970s. They pursued not only the original 40 miles, but also a larger 140-mile loop following ridge lines, rivers, and other natural features connecting more than thirty parks. In 2022, the network was nearly complete.[21]

The other great example is the Maricopa Trail, a 315-mile grand loop that runs entirely around the edges of Metropolitan Phoenix (figure 1.1). It was envisioned as a pedestrian beltway by the Maricopa County Parks and Recreation Department in 1997 and was completed in 2018. One of the reasons for building the trail was to highlight public awareness of the system of open spaces and regional parks along the outer edges of the greater Phoenix area. Portions of the trail, particularly where it runs

Figure 1.1. The Maricopa Trail, linking regional open spaces and parks surrounding Phoenix. (Credit: Courtesy of *Arizona Highways Magazine*)

through the larger open space preserves, are more rudimentary dirt-surfaced footpaths, with other sections following more formalized, paved canal maintenance paths. In some places where the loop trail passes through more urbanized areas, the trail follows sidewalks.[22]

Another example is the Vegas Valley Rim Trail, a 113-mile loop encircling greater Las Vegas (figure 1.2). Advocates envisioned it as "loop of trails and open space around our valley creating a buffer of recreation and protection of our spectacular Valley."[23] The idea grew out of the

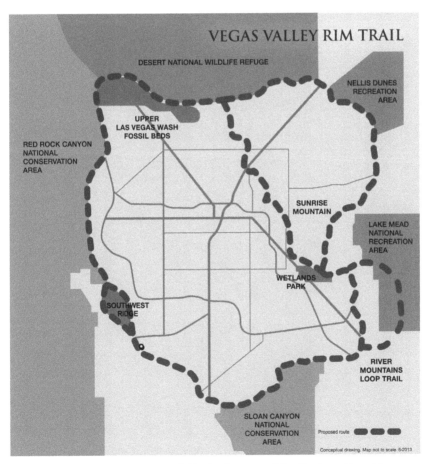

Figure 1.2. The Vegas Valley Rim Trail. (Credit: Courtesy of Get Outdoors Nevada)

2006 Regional Open Space Plan and has been pursued as a joint effort of the Outside Las Vegas Foundation and Southern Nevada Regional Planning Commission. As of 2022, this hiking and biking trail was more than 60 percent complete.[24]

Perhaps one of the most ambitious and extensive programs is the Carolina Thread Trail, a vast network of interconnected trails that will overlay fifteen counties and serve nearly three million people in two states (figure 1.3). That system envisions over 1,600 miles of trails, with

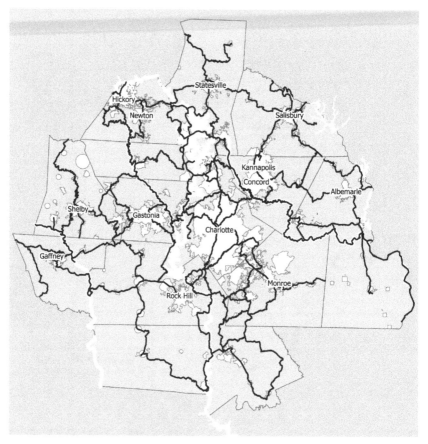

Figure 1.3. The Carolina Thread Trail in 2022. (Courtesy of the Carolina Thread Trail)

over 350 miles completed. The system includes several sections that could be called grand loop trails.

And finally, we look at the Transcarioca Trail in Rio de Janeiro. Though not yet an actual loop, this rim trail forms a 110-mile semicircular route that goes two thirds of the way around the city through wooded hills and jungle overlooking Rio de Janeiro. It connects seven of the city's parks along the way. It's touted as a place where you can "spend the day in the rainforest and be back in the concrete jungle for sunset beers." Built over a twenty-year period by volunteers, the project was the idea of Pedro Menezes, a flight attendant who on regular flights in and out of Rio noticed the line of green spaces, parks, and preserves and thought it would be easy to connect them.[25]

Town Walks

In most instances town walks consist largely of paved sidewalks, although other surfaces may be used, such as low-traffic walkable streets. Length can range from less than 2 miles to 6 miles or more. They are readily accessible and, ideally, branded with catchy and descriptive names including logos and prominently placed wayfinding "mile markers." There is a predictable level of quality to the route. Town walks offer a safe, pleasant experience, including smooth surfaces and adequate width for two people to walk side by side, and accommodate strollers and wheelchairs. They provide shade, lighting for night use, comfortable street crossings, and buffering from the street. Typically, they are landscaped with tree medians and have rest spots and other amenities. Town walks are not primarily utilitarian walking-as-transportation corridors, although many may be used that way. They are mostly for enjoyment. Although these pathways are predominantly loops, linear out-and-back routes are not categorically excluded.

Next, we look at the three subcategories of town walks.

Destination Walks

Destination walks are featured routes in cities. They are special corridors, primarily for walking, that offer more iconic experiences, cultural elements, historic spots, and other attractions that draw people from around the city and the region as well as tourists from other places. In some instances, they trace an important historic route. Some include bike paths on a separate tread.

There are several examples of destination trails, although they are not branded as such. These include the Indianapolis Cultural Trail and Boston's Freedom Trail. Asheville, North Carolina, also boasts its Urban Trail, a 1.7-mile walking loop through downtown with historic sites, intriguing architecture, shops and restaurants, and public art. And when completed, Denver's 5280 Trail (figure 1.4) will not only be a high-quality walking (and biking) route around central Denver, it will also become a major new overlay linear park transforming a 5-mile corridor in to a vibrant urban green space.[26, 27]

Community Walks

Community walks are attractive, typically branded, safe routes primarily for walking or running. They are strategically located to serve multiple neighborhoods and workplaces. They might be 2 to 6 miles in length to fit daily walking needs. Ultimately, like community parks, they should be prominent and easy to reach, within 1 to 3 miles of homes or workplaces.

In actuality, there are probably thousands of local walks that meet some or all of the characteristics defined here as community walks. One example is a fitness-through-walking program in the city of Matsumoto, Japan. In a 2014 *AARP Bulletin* article, Kirk Spitzer writes, "In

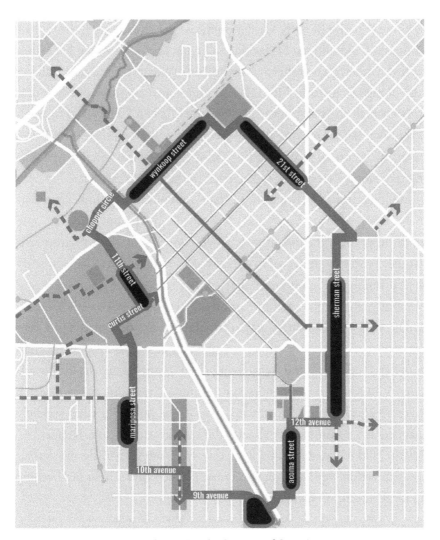

Figure 1.4. Denver's 5280 Trail map. (Credit: Courtesy of Civitas)

Matsumoto, officials have developed a network of more than 100 walking routes. . . . Even in winter clusters of residents can be seen walking along streets, parks, canals and around historic sites."[28]

Matsumoto was a great starting point, but there wasn't much more information about the actual routes, so I also looked for examples closer to home. Charlie Blosten, former public works director with the City of Littleton, Colorado, and I decided to go out and walk a couple of trails we had worked on together a few years back. We started out on a walking path along the historic City Ditch, a nineteenth-century aqueduct that runs through the heart of the city. We then turned and walked through downtown before picking up the greenway trail along the South Platte River. We returned to our starting point by following another connecting trail along a creek that linked back to the City Ditch path.

Looking at a map, we noticed that you could easily link these segments together into a very walkable 3-mile loop. Not only did our route go through the attractive historic downtown, it passed by a senior residential complex, connected to a recreation center, and had conveniently spaced restaurants and coffee shops along the way. It followed a very pleasantly landscaped corridor with shade trees, rest stops with benches, and flowing water in the river, the tributary creek, and the ditch. Along the way there were two attractive public gardens and an old cemetery with beautiful lawns and trees. Being close in, the route is readily available to hundreds of residences and businesses along its edges. Indeed, this trail checked every box except one. It was not branded or publicly mapped as a community walk and didn't have wayfinding signage. Yes, Charlie and I "created" this loop that day, but with little more than some direction signs and maybe a map posted online, it would become an ideal community walk for all.

Doorstep Walks

Doorstep walks are attractive neighborhood routes that anyone can enjoy daily, right outside the door, from home or the workplace. These too should be high-quality routes with good sidewalks, rest areas, landscaping, shade, and other amenities, easily reachable by residents. These are not specific branded routes. Rather, people can plot and vary their own routes. Although the length and layout are up to each person to determine, the goal is to encourage, broadly, at least twenty minutes of daily routine exercise. By implementing this class of walks, communities can adopt programs and policies that ultimately lead to widespread walkability everywhere, with an abundance of high-quality walking spaces.

This book does not focus on designing doorstep walk infrastructure. Walks out the door can be infinitely varied. But it advocates for the goal that, one day, walkability will be practically everywhere accomplished though effective policies. To that end, we can look at places that, by circumstance or intentional design, have great walkability. Rating services such as walkscore.com evaluate locales with set criteria that measure both the ability to access amenities such as shopping and streetscape conditions such as block length and pedestrian crossings. In North America, cities including New York, Vancouver, and San Francisco rank among the most walkable.[29] In addition, there are a number of planned communities where walkability has been written into the layout and design, with good sidewalks, landscaped tree medians, trails, and safe, easy-to-use street crossings (figure 1.5).

Besides looking at existing places with high walkability scores for lessons learned, we can also glean useful information from many places that are pursuing policies aimed at increasing their walkability. Several organizations host sites with resources, including Smart Growth America and the Pedestrian and Bicycle Information Center. At the forefront of policymaking are "complete streets" where communities pursue design standards that consider not only the movement of automobiles but also pedestrian and bicycle travel. According to Smart Growth America, more than 1,400 communities in the United States have adopted complete street policies, with Cleveland Heights, Ohio; Des Moines, Iowa; and Milwaukee, Wisconsin, leading the way.[30] So in thinking about doorstep walks, we can advocate for them by promoting

Figure 1.5. High-quality walk in a planned community. (Credit: Robert Searns)

the implementation of walkability policies and solutions such as complete street design.

Think of Them as a New Way of Walking

When we think about grand loops and town walks, we are talking about a new type of trail functionality. They are close-in places where people can primarily walk, run, hike, and trek (or ride a horse where appropriate). They bring increased access to outdoor places both in neighborhoods and in the hinterlands and invite visitors of varied genders, ages, and abilities. Cities can promote more routine use by planning them in ways in which people are encouraged, enabled, and motivated to enjoy them. Above all, the experience is key: what you see, smell, hear and feel along the way. When laying out routes there is particular attention to taking users through attractive environments in a pleasurable and safe way. We also want people to be able to afford to be there and feel welcomed there, regardless of economic means, race, or ethnicity. Finally, there is the goal of people being able to "travel light" with a daypack, not a heavy backpack. The chapters that follow will delve deeper into the types of grand loops and town walks and how to take them from concept to reality.

CHAPTER 2

Grand Loop Trails: Configurations and Themes

"A connected system of parks and parkways is manifestly far completer and more useful than a series of isolated parks."

—John and Frederick "Rick" Olmsted Jr., 1903

Julie George has run for decades both in town and on the trails winding through the foothills near her home in Denver, Colorado. Though leading a busy life as a mother and a professional, she runs four or more days a week. She says, "It's a fitness thing, a social thing, a chance to break away, a high!" Julie, like many runners, prefers surfaces that have some "give," like gravel or asphalt, as opposed to concrete, which doesn't flex. It's easier on the joints. She also mentioned that when she runs at night, she prefers the street to sidewalks because the streets tend to be lit, while the sidewalks are not. She says her trail run outings typically last an hour or two, and she prefers running loop trails because "you see something different the whole time."

Julie also mentioned potential interest in grand loops for organized running relays that can go a couple hundred miles or so. These events involve a team of 10–12 runners, doing rotating segments with support vans, typically over a twenty-four-hour period. The routes have hubs like restaurants or a Walmart lot en route. Some relays are supported by volunteers, and others are commercially operated. Companies such as Wildwest Runs and Ragnar Relays organize and support running relays.[1] She added that grand loops could be "ideal" for this type of activity.

There are likely to be many people—runners like Julie or walkers or strollers—who would welcome a grand loop around the growing city of Denver. A group of us tested out the concept, mapping out and walking a potential 100-plus-mile corridor around the metro area. Along the way, variability and the need for flexibility became quite evident. At times, we were hiking narrow dirt trails through rolling forested mountain terrain, and other times we crossed open prairie next to fenced ranchlands. Along some stretches, we followed existing suburban trails with varied widths and surfaces. Some were crushed gravel, and others were paved hike/bike paths. When there were no trails or other designated places to walk, we had to tread along back roads, although these were usually pleasant. It soon became evident that the shape would certainly not be a perfect circle or have a uniform type of tread. The route had to follow the undulations and irregularities of an amorphous metro edge. The key lesson was, depending on site conditions, surfaces, and landscape character, the alignment will meander and the characteristics will change. Indeed, there is no single grand loop shape or modality. They can manifest in multiple ways. Variations in the character and geometry are part of the picture.

Adapting to Conditions

I have defined a grand loop trail as a route along and around the perimeter of an urban area, mostly following the edge between city and countryside. It is created primarily for foot travel, though other uses may be considered. But as we learned from the Denver trek, the grand loop trail concept needs to be adaptable to local conditions such as the terrain and be adjusted for the particular opportunities, constraints, desires, and goals. This variability is a good thing, in that, with more flexibility and versatility, routes can be tweaked to best fit local conditions and highlight the unique aspects of any corridor. This factor can promote creativity and opportunities in envisioning and building them. Planners should collaborate with community advocates to tailor them to varied settings.

Indeed, in different cities, the layouts can have their own distinct characteristics that celebrate the unique aspects of a locale. For example, a grand loop trail around Los Angeles, where there is a mountain backdrop and the Pacific Ocean defining its edges, would be quite different from, say, one around Dallas, with its prairie and ranchland surroundings. Las Vegas has different defining edges, where there are mostly desert and federally owned open lands along that corridor. These significant swaths of public ownership and the iconic points of interest around Las Vegas highlight destinations like Red Rocks Canyon National Conservation Area and the Lake Mead National Recreation Area and create opportunities for carving out a trail right-of-way that conveys a distinct American desert theme. Those harsh, arid conditions also call for special features such as water refill stops and shade structures to ensure user safety and comfort. We can contrast these places with the environs around places like Boston, Portland, or Charlotte with their more verdant settings. In still other areas, constrains such as impassible terrain, difficult-to-access or blocked-off shorelines, and other factors like sprawling urbanization come into play.

In addition to the variations that determine the shape and suggest the preferred mode of use, such as walking, trekking, or biking, the special contextual characteristics of routes are equally significant. Because corridors are always multifaceted, the locale, geology, ecology, history, and culture create interpretive opportunities. The Denver route, for example, included not only varied types of trail surfaces and settings but also an array of defining local features, from unique geological formations to rusting old farm implements to bighorn sheep. In contrast, the Forest Park segment of Portland's 40-Mile Loop features a braided network of footpaths winding through dense woods with huge, gnarled, mossy alder, maple, and fir trees. A display at the trailhead introduces the ecological succession story you will experience as you walk the route. It describes how the landscape has evolved from grasslands of the past to the dense stands of large trees you see today, which will ultimately become an old-growth forest 250 years from now. On a potential grand loop in Sarasota, Florida, there is a segment called the Legacy Trail that recalls the circus trains P.T. Barnum once assembled, and in another locale you walk through subtropical wetlands home to alligators and colorful birds.[2] The message here is that grand loop trails can be infinitely varied. This can be important in planning them not only to provide a great trail but also to give each project its own identity, showcasing its special features.

In some regions, one urban area melds with another, or there is not an optimal route along the urban–rural interface. In places with these kinds of challenges, planning a grand loop trail requires even more flexibility and creativity. In these not-uncommon instances where the ideal open landscape terrain does not run all the way around a city, the solution may be a hybrid concept where the pathway runs partially on the urban–rural edge and partially through developed areas. The Phoenix Maricopa Trail is a good example of a hybrid grand loop where, in addition to the long stretches through desert wilderness, the trail occasionally winds through built-up, populated areas. In places, it even follows sidewalks and canal maintenance roads as it traverses several commercial and residential districts.

There are also the changes that occur over time that need to be anticipated. In plotting the Denver route, for example, it was evident in places that urbanization is rapidly expanding. We had to accept that some of the open areas we were enjoying at the time of our trek would probably be filled with houses and commercial development as the region continues to grow in population. No matter. There could be another concentric grand loop built farther out as the urbanized edges creep outward. The original loop would become a closer-in, urban trail and greenbelt, continuing to provide a major route and a right of way through those developing areas as the city expands.

Still, grand loop trails have defining commonalities. Most importantly, the route must optimize outstanding experiences, be readily accessible, and link green places together. It should strive to run mostly along the city–rural edges and typically offer a natural surface or gravel pathway. However, depending on local conditions such as environmental sensitivities, costs to build, and the availability of existing trails such as paved hike/bike segments that could close gaps, surface types and widths might vary.

Connections and Interconnections

Essential considerations in planning any trail or greenway, and especially a grand loop, are the concepts of *destinations* and *connectivity*. Another way to describe these is the notion of *places* and *links*, terms commonly used by urban designers. Simply put, a good route should take you somewhere, to a place, and the trail should, in a pleasing way, link places together. Grand loops focus on connecting and interconnecting destinations in multiple ways. When hiking a grand loop, the overall goal might be to complete the entire circuit, although the users may often have shorter distance goals of reaching places like a regional park or a scenic overlook. Grand loops typically also connect to other key nodes and destinations, from villages and hamlets to places of cultural, historic, or geological interest. They can also link to other trails, forming larger networks.

Both the Maricopa Trail encircling Phoenix and the Las Vegas Valley Rim Trail around Las Vegas emphasize connecting major parks and open spaces. The concept plan for a grand loop around Denver recommends connecting five state parks and multiple county open space parks. Portland, Oregon's 40-Mile Loop and the San Francisco area's 500+ mile Bay Trail link numerous parks, reserves, and other significant public green spaces.

Levels of Development

Unlike most paved greenways, grand loop trails can be designed to be functional at different stages of development, particularly when soft surface trails or improvised adaptations of low-traffic roads are used to form the loop. With this flexibility, a grand loop could be opened and enjoyed years before all the improvements are fully completed, or the trail may remain in a more rudimentary state.

At the optimal level, the entire loop is completed with a consistent high-quality tread, ideally 4 to 6 feet wide to accommodate side-by-side walking. There are no formidable barriers, and all road crossings are safe. At the next level, the entire loop is identified and defined, but there are less-than-optimal segments and fewer amenities such as trailheads or rest areas. In places the trail may be just a mowed strip through a field. At a more basic "starter level," the trail could be defined by wayfinding systems that might be as simple as a blaze on trees or posts and depicted on a map. Though not yet formal trails, the routes are identified and aligned to attract and serve a significant, albeit more adventurous segment of the population.

At an even more rudimentary level the routes are defined and established only informally in print or online. These are virtual grand loop trails. The loop might be created and posted by a public agency or delineated by individuals or laid out by trail guiding companies, perhaps revealed in posted blogs or articles. As a planner or trail advocate, you might start here by laying out and publicizing your own route. That's how a group of us first envisioned the Denver Grand Loop Trail.

In other instances, the route could be defined by an event such as an endurance race, a group walk, or even an organized multiday trek. Organizers could post temporary wayfinding markers tacked to trees or utility poles along with setting up special event road closures and temporary highway crossings to enable people to follow the route. Like the other wayfinding and virtual layout concepts, an event-defined route could be the starting point in identifying and promoting a more formal, established route in the future.

Regardless of the level of development, the corridor should be scouted and optimal routes and connections evaluated and marked. There should be no formidable barriers and no dead ends ever, and all road crossings and on-road segments must be safe. All or most of the route should be pleasant and easy to follow. The route layout should account for the potential for future upgrading over time.

Layouts and Shapes

With these adaptability considerations in mind, let's now look at a menu of very workable geometries. They represent different adaptations we can put into our grand loop vocabulary when thinking about varied local circumstances.

The Loop-around-the-City-Edge Template

We start with the generic layout concept where the grand loop trail forms a loop along the developed urban area edges. Figure 2.1 expresses the idea, although the actual shape will almost always undulate, sometimes significantly, depending on terrain and urbanization patterns. The Denver and Las Vegas loop concepts come closest to this prototype.

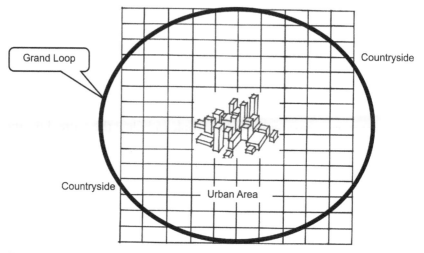

Figure 2.1. Prototypical grand loop. (Credit: Bill Neumann)

Hybrid

As discussed earlier, where urbanization patterns and other factors dictate, portions of the trail follow city edges and other segments follow in-town alignments. The Maricopa Trail around Phoenix is a good example. As always, the goal is to maintain a high-quality experience throughout. In chapter 8, we will imagine one of these in Sarasota, Florida. Figure 2.2 expresses this concept.

Hubs and Spokes: A Healing Wheel

In many cases it may be feasible, and desirable, to establish trail links that connect from city neighborhoods or city centers out to the grand loop on the edges of town. Ideally, these could follow greenways, trails,

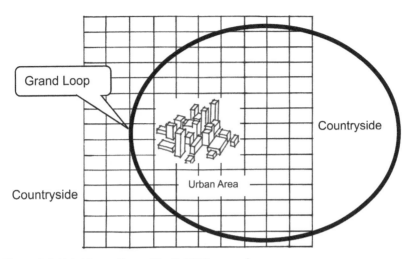

Figure 2.2. Hybrid grand loop. (Credit: Bill Neumann)

and other linear routes, forming spokes that tie central areas to the countryside. There could be a single hub, perhaps the downtown, or there could be multiple hubs depending on the configuration. I suggest the term *healing wheels* because this geometry could, by its shape and proximity to inner city areas, form an interconnected pathway system that promotes more convenient access to a larger network including the grand loop. This concept also greatly expands the options of types and lengths of trips. People could enjoy wedge trips by following the edges of the different slices of the pie shape that are created.

It creates an interconnected pathway network, making it easier for more people to readily access places to recreate and find solace. Additionally, the wheel helps make urban landscapes greener. Of course, the wedge shapes are not literal. In reality, they would be much more amorphous, but still this pattern suggests a template that could be useful and should be considered in planning almost any regional trail system. A concept is shown in figure 2.3.

George Rasmussen, a senior hiking group leader living near Denver, loves this idea. He said he and his wife hiked the entire 567-mile

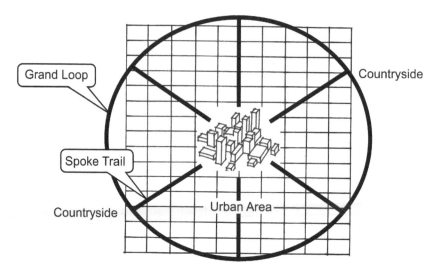

Figure 2.3. Hub and spokes (the "healing wheel"). (Credit: Bill Neumann)

Colorado Trail through the Rockies without camping. They made 10-
to 20-mile daily walks along the length of the trail, shuttling by car from
point to point each day. Based on that experience, he said he sees the
feasibility of this. "It would be a lot easier along a grand loop—including hiking wedges—because each day someone could pick you up, making it easy to sleep at home each night."

Concentric and Multilayered

Like the pattern of urban freeways that form as cities expand outward,
there can be concentric grand loop trails. The newer loop would define
the current urban edge, and like a closer-in freeway loop, the original
grand loop would still be there and serve a vital purpose. There could be
hybrid connections as well, where older parts of routes connect with the
newer layers. Ultimately, concentric systems can evolve into networks
with multiple route lengths, convenient points of access, and experience
possibilities. A concept is shown in figure 2.4.

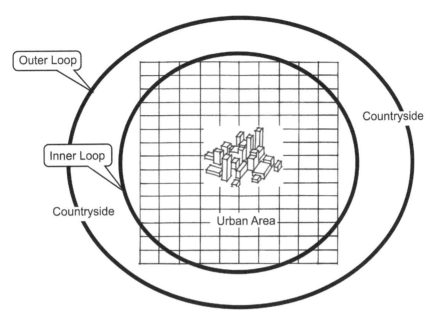

Figure 2.4. Concentric loops. (Credit: Bill Neumann)

Attached Subloops

The concept calls for attaching shorter (e.g., 3- to 6-mile) loops hanging off a grand loop, forming a daisy chain. Figure 2.5 illustrates this concept. Some of these could be more rural trail loops and others town walks that access neighborhoods proximate to the grand loop. Mountain bikers have also suggested that this layout concept could serve the biking community. As a Casper, Wyoming, mountain biking advocate suggested, the subloops envisioned in this geometry could be destination biking venues. There could also be subloops designated for equestrian uses. This configuration provides yet another opportunity for expanded access and enjoyment by diverse groups.

Of course, in some instances, depending on local preferences, the entire grand loop and subloop system could be opened to bikes or equestrians. This is the case with the Maricopa Trail. According to Outdoor Industry Association, there are about 4.3 million equestrians on

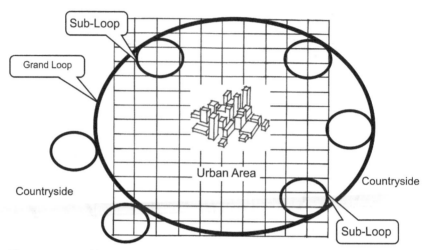

Figure 2.5. Grand loop with subloops. (Credit: Bill Neumann)

trails in the United States, about 7 percent of the users.[3] Jan Hancock, a lifelong equestrian and an author of *The Equestrian Guide Handbook*, advises that when thinking about this mode of use we need to consider a number of factors, such a space for horse trailer unloading with an adequate turn radius, hitching facilities, and water.[4] Jan thinks that grand loops would be a great asset for equestrians, with potential for both day rides and multiday treks. Not only would horse owners benefit, but tour companies could organize rides so anyone could participate. "It would be a great way to see places," she says. She added that she likes the idea of shorter loops—maybe 6 miles—attached to grand loops.

"Baby Grand" Loops

These are much shorter loops that encircle smaller towns. Rather than being 50 to 200 miles in length encircling metro areas, these might run from less than 10 to maybe 20 miles long. Once example is the Key West Cycling Route, a part of the Florida Overseas Heritage Trail. It runs for about 10 miles around the perimeter of Key West, Florida—though I should note that this route is primarily touted as a bike path.[5] Nonetheless, it demonstrates the concept of baby grand loop geometry.

Forming Interconnected Metro-Wide Networks

Grand loops, town walks, greenways, and other urban trails could also be woven into expansive interconnected networks. These networks could link grand loops, town walks, and other trails and greenways, including trail spokes that extend from urban centers and downtown areas to the outer edges.

Even Grander Trail Systems

Grand loops around cities can be interconnected and woven into even larger systems. This includes creating more extensive systems that tie into much larger trails that cross states and even continents. At first, this might seem almost unfathomable, but the reality is that there are projects in several places where these are being pursued.

In *Greenways for America*, Charles Little describes forming networks of greenways where greenways, trails, and parks are tied together into larger regional networks and even bigger systems traversing states and provinces.[6] Others have also had this grand network vision, including Warren Manning, who around 1919 called for a national network of "commercial and recreation areas and connecting ways." He described "a system so devised as to enable all the people to find a place near their homes where well-organized, low-cost transportation, camping and food supply facilities, will enable them to take frequent advantage of it."[7]

Grand loops could access major long-distance trails such as the Appalachian Trail, the East Coast Greenway, Canada's Bruce Trail, New York's Erie Canal Trail, and the Pacific Crest Trail—to name a few—and many other state, provincial, and national scale routes. In addition, projects like the 1,500-mile Sun Corridor Trail, being pursued in the American Southwest, envision linking cities and grand loops together. That trail will connect the Phoenix Maricopa Trail to the Las Vegas Valley Loop Trail.[8] Like interstate highways and urban beltways, grand loops can be connected into much larger networks.

Accommodating Different Types of Trips, Trip Length, and Travel Times

The grand loop concept is intended to reach a broad cross-section of people, abilities, and preferences. To do this, grand loops should be designed to allow a range of travel options. Because they run mostly along the edges of a city, visitors can choose from multiple access points and trip lengths, custom tailoring their visits to address time availability, capabilities, hiking with young children, and other considerations. Outings can range from day hikes to multiday treks. An important part of this concept is establishing convenient points of access, including trailheads, within a half day's walk of each other.

Types of Trips

One of the appealing, unique features of grand loop trails is that, by being close in but still on the edge, they can accommodate all kinds of visits and hiker objectives. A key attribute is the ability to travel light. This is a growing movement in the trail community. At the core of this movement is the idea of carrying just a daypack, not a heavy backpack. Unlike an overnight backcountry trip where a backpack is needed to carry gear, on a grand loop trek, with a little bit of planning and efficient packing, you need only a daypack to carry necessities. This is facilitated by points of access and venues with amenities such as toilets, lodging, and convenience stores, which I call "service nodes," an important part of grand loop planning. We want to lay out the route with strategic placement and ensure that these places are accessible and convenient to hikers.

Following are some key types of trips that users can take on grand loops, all while traveling light.

Day Trips

These are probably the most common types of visit: walking a segment of the loop or, if available, walking around an attached subloop. These can initially encourage people to experience a grand loop and then inspire many to plan longer treks. Indeed, some may choose to work their way around a grand loop with a series of consecutive day visits, just as we walked around Denver. Agencies or advocacy groups might want to create "trekking passports" that motivate people to engage by checking off completed segments.

Wedge Trips

As described earlier, using a spoke-and-rim system, visitors could plot wedge treks, starting in the central city, trekking out to the rim, following the rim to the next spoke, and returning back to town. These kinds of expeditions can be taken in many ways. One can walk the entire wedge route that might be a 30- or 40-mile trip. This could be a two- or three-day trip, perhaps staying in lodging in the service node areas along the way. Alternatively, one can complete the trip in a day on a mountain bike. You can ride a bike share out to the edges, walk the grand loop segment, and return home on a bike share. There are lots of options and mode possibilities. Think flexibility! Another nice feature is that people can schedule multiple subsequent wedge trips over time, working their way around the entire grand loop. Wedge routes could be a tourism opportunity for travelers staying in the city—a way to really immerse themselves in the place they are visiting.

A Multiday "Pilgrimage"

The granddaddy of treks is committing to walk the entire circle. That trip might be a single outing spending nights on the trail along the way. Or it could be series of day trips, returning home each night by transit or ride service or other combinations to complete the entire journey.

Highlighting Thematic Features

A grand loop trail planner may decide to designate a theme or set of themes for their trail. It might be a cultural, historic, or ecological narrative or highlight a special feature, such as a seashore. Maybe the theme is about connecting the regional parks around the edges of a city, as the Maricopa Trail planners envisioned. There could be themes for different segments of a single grand loop as well. For example, a loop around Sarasota might highlight the marine features of the Gulf of Mexico along one segment and the Florida wetland habitats along another part. Highlighting a theme can generate publicity for the trail and encourage broader use.

Greenbelt, Conservation, and Urban Shaping

Ideally all grand loop projects seek to preserve visual landscapes and have ecological conservation missions in addition to promoting trail use. This includes not only careful, sustainable, environmentally sensitive trail design but also preserving the corridor that the trail passes through. Indeed, in this scenario, the trail can become the armature of a much wider greenbelt. The trail theme could emphasize this feature with proactive open space acquisitions, scenic easements, interpretive or educational displays, and volunteer stewardship projects.

The Appalachian Conservancy offers a great model for this, proactively working to preserve landscapes and vistas along the famed Appalachian Trail route. Indeed, conservation-themed grand loops could inspire better urban shaping by preserving prominent green spaces along the edges in the spirit of Ebenezer Howard's greenbelt vision.[9]

"Pilgrimage" Trekking and Healing

In my planning practice, when we were envisioning a grand loop trail encircling the town of Silverthorne, Colorado, one participant in a public meeting stood up and suggested that we place trailside stupas (Buddhist meditational structures) at strategic points along the route where people could stop and meditate. Certainly, this is not unknown. Japan's Kumono Kodo has small shrines along the way. Similarly, they are along the Camino de Santiago. Though not grand loops per se, these trails have a mindful journey narrative that is a big part of their heritage and their attraction with shrines and places of worship along the way. In this scenario, meditative spaces would be carefully integrated into the trail planning and design. For example, a meditative space might be a bench and an arbor that overlooks a calming view. While keeping separation of church and state, there certainly could be opportunities to create nondenominational meditative spots at strategic points along our trails. This theme could also serve groups suffering from posttraumatic stress disorder and other stresses and traumas, such as veterans' groups recovering from combat situations and first responders and healthcare workers heavily burdened by pandemics.

Historic, Cultural, and Ecological Interpretation

Grand loops can serve a specific educational or interpretive focus with displays, artifacts, and routing that reflect the unique character of the place. In addition, the routes can be programmed to encourage educational access by school groups who might visit both to hike and to work on volunteer stewardship projects. There can also be special conservation sites along the way where adult volunteers work on restoration projects.

Tourist Destination Both Locally and from Afar

Finally, we can talk about drawing visitors from near and far, laying out loops as a destination, showcasing a city or region's special geographic, historic, or cultural aspects. Denver can emphasize its Rocky Mountain backdrop, Las Vegas its desert landscapes, and Rio De Janeiro its close-in jungle highlands. The possibilities are limitless as each place highlights its own special features and characteristics. This can certainly help build the case for grand loops as a significant economic generator.

This chapter has laid a comprehensive profile of what grand loops are and what they can be. Certainly, there is room for other scenarios and variations on this concept. The commonality is that they are on the city edges, offer multiday trekking opportunities, and form a complete loop. The next chapter takes a similar look at town walks, the smaller companion and the other half of the city trails and walking routes picture.

CHAPTER 3

Town Walks: Configurations and Themes

"I started walking around my neighborhood more. Compared
with those wild places, this was unremarkable . . . But . . .
I listened. I felt. . . And . . . the neighborhood came alive . . .
in a way that those mountaintops . . . never had."

—Francis Sanzaro, "The Next Walk You Take Could
Change Your Life"[1]

Dru Carroll strolls nearly every day. It's her morning routine. She started decades ago in her native Boston, walking in rain, shine, and snow. Once she retired from her job, she moved to sunny Tucson, Arizona. Now Dru sets out from her doorstep at 7 a.m. each morning, to beat the heat, for a 2-mile stroll with her beagle, Lucy. Her route follows a low-traffic street in the hills overlooking the city, and she adds distance by going in and out of cul-de-sacs along the main road. The course runs through rolling terrain with intimate views of all manner of cacti and the downtown skyline in the background. There are no sidewalks, but one could argue that with only occasional cars, the street here is perfectly adequate.

Typically, her walks take about forty-five minutes. "Sometimes I turn left at the bottom of the drive and sometimes right depending on my whim on any given day." She says she likes the gentle grades. They add a bit more resistance to her steps. She enjoys the invigoration of the morning desert air seasoned by the local flora. "Often, I meet friends and neighbors who also follow the route, so it's also a great way to socialize a bit. It's always the first thing before I do my morning stuff."

I asked her whether she ever tires of the regimen, and she says, "No, and in fact, I've been doing this for decades. It's easy to do every day!" She recalls her 2-mile commute in Boston. Unlike her current neighborhood, "in Boston traffic you had to have sidewalks."

"It was my way to get energized in the morning and relieve stress in the afternoon. And a way to organize my thoughts," Dru recalls. She said she's read that repetitive movement like walking helps promote creative thinking and recall.

Fortunately, Dru found her walking corridors right outside her door. Many places don't have that amenity. Our planning goal is to bring safe, comfortable, pleasant places to walk to many more people. At the basic level it's about communities pursuing walkability policies.

After taking the exploratory grand loop trek around the edge of metro Denver that I laid out in the Prologue, I decided to test out the town walks concept in earnest. I picked out routes of different lengths from 2 to 10 miles through areas of different US cities to see how I'd do. I tested routes in center city neighborhoods and in the suburbs, and I even walked the proposed 5-mile 5280 Trail loop around downtown Denver. I took loop walks through planned communities in several cities, walked a route near the World Trade Center in lower Manhattan, and tried a loop that included a walkable segment of quartz sand beach on Siesta Key in Florida. In many instances I walked where there were no sidewalks, and I had to walk in the street. I also tried taking a route from a transit stop in another part of town to see what that was like.

Each walk had its own special features and pleasures. There were parks, shops, and sometimes a yard with a beautifully planted garden. On one walk there was an impromptu blues concert in a neighborhood park, and on another were street musicians with an open guitar case to receive what you wanted to contribute. Some walks had little free libraries, set up by residents, where you could trade a book. I learned from this experimentation that are multiple ways to envision and configure town walks—different sizes, shapes, and ambiances. This chapter explores some of the workable possibilities.

Connections and Interconnections

Returning to the definition in chapter 1, we recall three types of town walks: destination walks, which are citywide attractions; community walks, which serve neighborhoods; and doorstep walks, which each person can plot out their front door. Like grand loop trails, there are multiple ways these town walks can be configured, themed, and linked into their communities.

Regardless of the shape or theme, ideally, there is convenient, abundant access to town walks from doorsteps, workplaces, and lodging. Everyone should be able to reach a town walk easily via a safe, comfortable route, on foot, on bike, or via a short transit ride. If we compare suggested travel distances (on foot) to traditional parks, we can look at several studies for guidance. In a *Trust for Public Land* piece, "How Far to Your Nearest Park?," Peter Harnik and Jeff Simms suggest that parks should be between 1/8 and 1 mile away from every home.[2] Based on this standard and putting it in terms of the time it takes to access these on foot, I propose making it convenient enough to promote routine use—within five to ten minutes of every doorstep.

Although town walks are primarily for recreation and fitness, whenever practical they should also serve as routes to destinations such as parks, shops, civic centers, schools, and points of interest. When near schools, these loops could serve as places to stroll or exercise, which can benefit students and faculty. Adding an educational dimension to this, school administrators I have talked with suggest that students could adopt segments where they plant trees in the medians or help with upkeep projects. There may also be opportunities for children to plant fruit trees or vegetable gardens in the medians along the walks.

Having readily accessible systems of town walks within five or ten minutes of everyone is a tall order, but pursuing safe, equitable access to trails from all neighborhoods needs to be a priority in the planning. As more town walks are designed in more centralized locations, plans should address access from transit and bike routes and consider providing parking spots at access points for people traveling to destination walks where appropriate. Some communities enhance this access by connecting walkable links that tie into the surrounding areas. The town walks in Denver and Indianapolis represent this model with linkages to surrounding neighborhoods. These connections greatly expand the service area.

In some instances, access points may be subtle, known only to the locals. In other places, where neighborhoods are less intimate, there should be prominently marked trailheads or "gateway nodes" that serve as entry points. They may be marked by clearly visible signs or an architectural feature such as an attractive trellis, as illustrated in figure 3.1. Ideally route maps will be posted at access points. (See chapter 4 for more details.)

Levels of Development

As for grand loop trails, there are different levels of development for town walks depending on the extent of the resources a community is prepared to invest. They range from fully improved high-end walks to

Figure 3.1. Town walk trailhead. (Credit: Bill Neumann)

less developed pathways to improvised, do-it-yourself and temporarily established walks. It's important to emphasize, as was the case with grand loops, that because of the inherent flexibility of travel on foot, town walk facilities can be functional at almost any level of development, and less improved projects can be upgraded later as more resources become available. They don't have to be fully built out before you can cut the ribbon as long as they are safe and pleasant, and people can easily use them. Let's consider five levels of development.

High-End Town Walks

These are branded, fully improved, landscaped, readily accessible, high-quality pedestrian pathways. These are the ideal walking routes. They have smooth, level, off-street walking surfaces, pedestrian-friendly street crossings, landscaped medians, and tree canopy shading convenient rest areas, benches, and shelters. There is easy-to-follow wayfinding, and there are other amenities such as coffee shops and restaurants. They often link parks and other civic spaces together. They are, in effect, overlaid pedestrian parks integrated into the community fabric. Denver's 5280 Trail and the Indianapolis Cultural Trail are good examples.

More Basic Town Walks

At the next, less costly level are functional corridors that offer safe, pleasant routes. Like the more deluxe examples in Denver and Indianapolis, these are officially designated and branded projects. They have good wayfinding and safe, easy street crossings, and they connect desirable places, but they are not yet fully improved. Amenities such as tree medians and rest areas may not be consistent along the way. In some places people may need to walk on-street where there is little traffic and car travel is at low speeds. These may be carved out to establish an initial corridor with the intent of upgrading them in the future. The Turquoise Trail in Tucson, which is defined primarily by a painted strip on the sidewalks, is a good example.

Rudimentary Town Walk Routes

These are bare-bones but functional routes defined primarily by simple wayfinding such as blazes on light posts. There is often an online map. The sidewalks are in good or fair condition, and there are safe street crossings. These routes are also interesting and pleasant places to walk. These can be a first step to getting the idea out there. They can be a demonstration of concept where, working with existing conditions, planners can create a basic corridor that suggests a route with the intent of future upgrading.

Improvised Walks

There are also do-it-yourself walks that individuals or communities create on their own. One example that stood out for me is a 2.6-mile loop through Cedar Hills Oregon, a middle-income community near Portland. Originally platted in the late 1940s, Cedar Hills has about two thousand 1950s-vintage single-family ranch homes with a diverse mix of residents. Kristin Preston, a resident and routine walker, graciously offered to show me her improvised doorstep route. We started out walking on the road along a pleasant tree-lined collector street accessible to much of the neighborhood via side streets. I expected to see cars, but instead the traffic consisted of a parade of neighbors walking down the middle of the road. It was a promenade. There was a woman with a dog, a couple pushing a stroller, and others simply out for a stroll. Clearly a lot of people had the same idea that morning. As we greeted people it became evident that this was also a social event.

About a third of the way into the walk, there was a hidden little section of sidewalk that ran between two houses. We cut through, crossed a local street, and turned onto another hidden sidewalk. That walk morphed into a foot trail that meandered through a wooded grove and led to a neighborhood park with a path, then a causeway with a lake on one side and a marshland with red-winged blackbirds and ducks on the other. Along the way to the park, we greeted some birdwatchers who pointed out the rare find they spotted with their binoculars. After rounding the lake, we looped back to the very walkable street grid and made our way back to Kristin's house. Although Kristin's walk was not officially planned, it was a safe, pleasant, and interesting route.

Temporal Walks

Town walks can also include temporarily designated routes for special events. These could be formed by closing streets or limiting auto traffic for the duration of the event. The walk might be a one-time occurrence, a regularly scheduled Sunday street market, a "First Friday" art fair, or a seasonal setup. The seminal book *Tactical Urbanism* offers a number of techniques for neighborhoods creating their own walking improvements, often with some street paint and bollards.[3] Cyclovia is a well-established model for temporary routes, although these are usually officially sanctioned events. These originated in Bogotá, Colombia, where streets were closed on Sundays for biking and walking. Cities all over the world now host them. They are usually festive, with street vendors and entertainment.

Shared streets are an example of a transitional town walk technique that has the potential to become permanent. During the COVID-19 pandemic, several cities, including Boston, Minneapolis, Oakland, Burbank, and Denver, temporarily closed local, low-traffic blocks, creating "shared streets" for safer outdoor gathering.[4,5] In Oakland, officials established a "slow streets" program with the "aim of making a network of neighborhood streets more safe, slow, comfortable, and fun for all road users, encourage residents to use their streets as community space, and improve pedestrian safety at key locations where people are likely to be walking." Unfortunately, Oakland later cut back on the program, citing local residents' concerns about convenient automobile access and the lack of permanence of some of the slow street barriers.[6,7] Other places, though, are still pursuing them. In Queens, Brooklyn, and Denver, officials considered permanently continuing shared streets on some blocks after the pandemic.[8–10]

Town Walk Layouts and Shapes

Town walk geometry can vary depending on the city fabric they wind through and the objectives of the project. There can be many shapes with multiple opportunities to connect with other trails or uses. This list of four possible configurations is a starting point; variations will emerge and the list will broaden as trends and technology change.

Freestanding

This is the basic loop concept (figure 3.2). These loops can be in core city areas, in suburbs or suburban areas, and in some instances attached to larger grand loop trails, as described in chapter 2. They can be built from scratch in a new development or overlaid on an existing street grid but not attached to existing trails. Although the length of town walks can vary, in the case of longer (e.g., 5- to 6-mile) loops, there can be smaller subloops incorporated into the pattern to serve those who choose a shorter walk and to offer more variety in the routes people can take (figure 3.3).

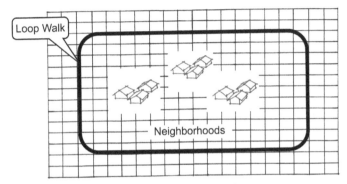

Figure 3.2. Freestanding loop. (Credit: Bill Neumann)

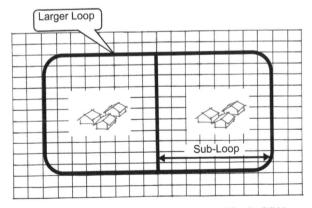

Figure 3.3. Freestanding loop with optional shorter loop. (Credit: Bill Neumann)

Attached to Greenways or Other Urban Trails

Town walks can be tied to greenways or other urban trails by incorporating sections of those linear trails into their loops. This version can expand trail options and provide enhanced access to greenways, other trail systems, and parks. The Cedar Hills walk does this by connecting into a trail that runs through Commonwealth Park. There can also be a whole chain of attached loops along a larger greenway. This concept is shown in figure 3.4.

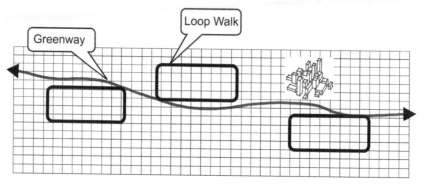

Figure 3.4. Loops attached to a linear trail. (Credit: Bill Neumann)

Attached to Transit Lines

Another interesting opportunity is to connect town walk loops to transit line stops where a person could hop a bus or a train, get off at a desired stop or station, and use that place as a point of departure, picking up a loop that starts and ends at that stop. Figure 3.5 illustrates this concept. A loop might even connect to two or more stations or stops. In this case a walker could disembark at one stop, walk the along the loop to the next station, reboard, and close the loop by riding the bus or train back to where they got off. The key is identifying good points of embarkation along transit lines where you can lay out a great walk anchored by the station.

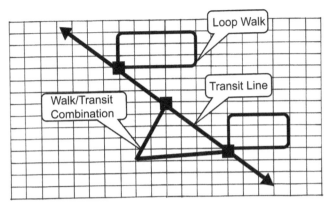

Figure 3.5. Loops attached to a transit route. (Credit: Bill Neumann)

Connected to Grand Loops

Town walks can offer enhanced local access to the grand loop system, expand hiking options for longer-distance grand loop trekkers, and enable shorter hikes that sample a segment of a larger grand loop. (See figure 2.5 in chapter 2.)

The routes can intersect, or they may be tied together with easy-to-follow five- to ten-minute linking spurs. An interconnecting network of town walks would create a metro-wide regional pedestrian park. It can extend for miles. Tie in a grand loop trail along the city edges and you have quite a system! Communities, and even metro regions, could boast interconnected green overlay systems. Special wayfinding maps posted along trails at entry points can guide users who want to trek this larger system.

Theme-Based Walks

Like grand loop trails, a town walk can be theme oriented. It can be interpretive, educational, cultural, historical, artistic, or another specialized theme. It can be an art walk with displays, sculptures, or murals.

The theme can showcase historic buildings and monuments or other unique features. There can be a performing arts theme with mini-stages for musicians, poets, or actors. Walks can focus on local cultural aspects such as ethnic restaurants, craft shops, and galleries.

Theme-based walks can be located to reveal the characteristics of a certain significant area. The Turquoise Trail highlights the original settlement of Tucson and its old barrios. Asheville, North Carolina, has The Architecture Trail, a walk that showcases its early twenti-eth-century buildings. Thematic walks might tend to be more centrally located, although they can be found in specific neighborhoods, such as a studio loft district or a microbrewery area. Either way, there would be local and citywide draws. Walking tours can certainly be a part of the picture, with wayfinding signage, hired or volunteer guides, or mobile apps. The Turquoise Trail has a great guide-led tour program. I was advised by one volunteer that "it's good to book early because the walks are extremely popular!"

Once themed routes are created, they can be promoted to draw both locals and tourists. There are already many interpretive or themed walks posted online in cities worldwide. Typically, merchant's associa-tions organize them. These can be year-round, seasonal, on weekends, or as special events. Atlanta, Georgia, offers multiple street art walks, and myriad other themed walks are available in Beijing, Amsterdam, and Melbourne.[11] This genre also includes sidewalk events that are now virtually everywhere, with art displays, musicians, and cuisine to sample.

Use Preferences

> *"As the trails and hiking community becomes more inclusive of people of all ages, abilities and cultures, urban hikes are an important opportunity so many people can enjoy. You don't need*

a car, special equipment, or anything more than the willingness to take a nice walk. Walks like this are pure joy and are possible wherever you live."

—Jeff Olson,[12] trail planner and author of *The Third Mode: Toward a Green Society*

Town walks are primarily for walking. However, as for grand loops, there can be a range of potential uses, including running, biking, and other modes such as scooters and skates. In the case of town walks, it is especially important that user conflicts be avoided. Increasingly there have been conflicts between pedestrians and scooters, especially the powered models. Sometimes regulations address the problem by keeping bikes and scooters off designated sidewalks, although enforcement is not always successful and there is not enough safe on-street bike infrastructure. Planning for town walks must take the potential for multiple uses into account and address the issue of conflicts between bikes and pedestrians. Although awareness of this issue has been somewhat lacking, increasingly advocates and designers are pursuing solutions that strive to separate uses.

Town Walks as Transformative Infrastructure

"Urban Forests can be defined as networks or systems . . . groups of trees . . . forests . . . street trees, trees in parks and gardens, and . . . in derelict corners. Urban forests are the backbone of the green infrastructure . . . ameliorating a city's environmental footprint."

—Food and Agriculture Organization of the United Nations[13]

Like greenways, town walks are adaptive and transformative green infrastructure. As Charles Little stated, greenways are "based primarily on regional landforms" from "urban rivers" to "ecological corridors," and they have succeeded phenomenally in connecting people to natural and geological features and have helped to preserve and rehabilitate these spaces in cites. Although traditional greenways and many urban parks are important green spaces in cities, for the most part they are site-specific places that most city dwellers must travel to. Because they can overlay the human-built cityscape of sidewalks and streets, town walks take this vision to a new level by greening the broader urban grid.

Like grand loops, as we saw in the previous chapter, town walks can serve two important overarching functions. They provide high-quality places to walk, and they can significantly reshape and enhance the natural landscapes of cities. Like grand loop trails, properly designed town walks can become "armatures of green," lined with trees, shrubs, grasses, and flowers. When you look at a healthy city from the air, you'll often see expanses of vegetation in addition to the rooftops. Some use the term *urban forests* to describe this leafy layer. Landscaped town walks can link together and expand these vegetated areas, which not only beautify but also provide habitat for many species from bees to nesting birds. Along with walkability, an important goal of town walks is to enhance this green network. In the following chapters we will look at ways to effectively plan the grand loop and town walk configurations and geometries described above.

CHAPTER 4
Guiding Principles and Attributes

"Trail quality matters because your trail is part of a competitive marketplace. . . . People 'vote with their feet' by selecting routes with a good reputation."

—Amy Camp, *Deciding on Trails*[1]

In envisioning and planning grand loops and town walk routes, it is important to have guidelines to set a standard of quality for what will be built and a comprehensive list of attributes to consider. These are the guardrails for planning enjoyable, safe, buildable, and maintainable projects. You may want to modify and embellish these guidelines to best suit your project and community.

The list of guiding principles in this chapter is a starting point. There are multiple resources to turn to when drafting guiding principles. These include trail and pedestrian master plans published by many jurisdictions and agencies. They're easily found online. For planning grand loops, one of the better publications is the *2019 Toronto Trails Strategy Plan*. It provides a great framework and the right mindset to lay out projects.[2] For town walks, an online document titled "SF Better Streets: A Guide for Making Street Improvements in San Francisco" is a handy resource.[3] See also "Sidewalks and Shared-Use Paths," published by the University of Delaware, and "Principles of Pedestrian Planning," published by the Institute for Planning and Development Policy.[4]

Overall the goal should be to envision and promote the project as part of a long-term urban shaping effort providing opportunities for everyone, preserving open spaces, protecting vistas, and promoting economic development. It should create a multigenerational legacy that leaves behind greenbelts that define the edges of cities and high-quality urban spaces in town that promote a happier, healthier population.

Ten Guiding Principles

1. Provide a high-quality experience.
2. Offer high-quality amenities.
3. Install effective wayfinding.
4. Prioritize safety and security.
5. Plan for easy access and connectivity.
6. Be a good neighbor.
7. Promote stewardship and environmental awareness.
8. Plan projects that are sustainable and affordable to build and maintain.
9. Strive for inclusivity and tolerance with diverse equitable access.
10. Create a legacy resource.

Planning attributes are the important contextual elements of a pathway for determining the best alignment and pursuing best practices in fitting the trail or walk into its setting. They should be addressed and refined from the vision stage through the planning process. Attributes shape the trail experience and frame the opportunities, challenges, and constraints in designing a project. The list includes such items as ambience and field conditions, accessibility and linkage opportunities, and cultural context. Other factors that may affect routing and the character of a hike or walk are important. Like guiding principles, the attributes provide a mental checklist for taking the vision to the next level. Attributes vary by location. There are remote areas as well as busy urban areas to consider.

Base data can be gleaned in multiple ways. Check with local land managers, mapping and data management departments, planners, and other officials. Also contact law enforcement, fire, and rescue personnel. Asking the locals such as the people who walk or hike in the area, shopkeepers, and area residents is helpful as well. Of course, going out and walking the prospective route is an essential part of the assessment, including going out at different times of year and different times of day.

The following is list of key attribute considerations. They are grouped by category. This list is a starting point. There are many published resources with more detailed trails and urban walks guidance listed under "Helpful Resources" at the end of this book.

Quality of the Experience

These attributes focus on the human aspect, considering who will use the facility, how they will use it, and the quality of the experience.

Who Will Use the Trail, and How Will They Use It?

Who will be the likely visitors, and how will they enjoy the corridor? How can more people be invited to use the trail? Plan to accommodate a broad cross-section of users, including a diverse range of ethnic, racial, and income groups.

Ambiance

What is sensory character of the route? In addition to the views, what are the sounds and scents along the way? How does it feel to be there? Consider both the interesting and monotonous factors.

Scenic Values and Views

In aligning a route, evaluate the scenic values, views, and key overlook spot potentials. Consider both close-in aesthetic features and the long vistas. This includes perhaps a mountain ridgeline or pastoral landscape. Look for iconic features such as a striking geological formation along a grand loop or an architectural facade on a town walk. Are there opportunities to highlight and showcase a desirable element? Note views to avoid, such as a mining or road scar or a blighted area in town. Identify potential overlook sites. These can be destinations along a walk. Note vulnerable landscapes that may need protection in the future.

Climate and Weather

Assess weather patterns and climate character to best ensure user comfort. Is the area arid? Does it get extremely hot or cold? Where might shade or shelters be needed? Is the area prone to frequent violent storms? What about temperatures in the different seasons? Will snow and ice be an issue? What about snow plowing; where does the removed snow go?

This analysis involves assembling weather charts that show, typically by month, temperature and precipitation patterns. Park managers and street department personnel may also be helpful in advising on weather impacts. This information can aid in plotting routes to avoid disruption by snow or rising creeks and to avoid harsh exposed areas.

User Comforts and Amenities

Consider two types of amenities. First there are the fixtures and furnishings, such as rest areas, toilets, tables, benches, overlooks, and, in some instances, spaces for camping. Where are the best places to locate these? Toilets and drinking water are critical, and they should be readily available, especially at trailheads. Chemical toilets are the most cost-effective; other options include plumbed and self-composting devices. The facility should be wheelchair accessible, and a simple architectural frame can help better fit the structure into the surroundings. They should not be placed near residences, dining places, or other incompatible locations. Regarding drinking water, although many walkers carry their own, dehydration is always a concern. Having a potable water tap wherever feasible is desirable, particularly on grand loops. Both drinking water and toilet facilities should be strategically placed.

Second, where are potential service nodes with convenience stores, restaurants, and lodging? How far apart are they? What is the best routing that enables convenient access to amenities along the way? Ideally on grand loop trails, the alignment is planned to access commercial amenities every 10 to 12 miles. On town walks they would be conveniently located within a five- or ten-minute walk. Cellular service in more remote areas is also a consideration.

Rest areas are places to stop, recoup, look at a map, take in a view, have a drink or snack, and rest (figure 4.1). They are a must! Properly designed and placed, they are the seasoning of the trail or walk experience—a reward for completing a segment. They should be conveniently and strategically placed. On grand loops they might be a mile apart and at key viewpoints. In town, they're maybe a quarter mile apart. It's also good to place rest stops at key junctions such as trail intersections and at the tops of hills, where reaching it is a reward for making the ascent.

The settings should be comfortable, with shade, shelter from wind and rain, and noise buffering.

Figure 4.1. Rest area and overlook. (Credit: Bill Neumann)

Benches and Tables

A bench rests the mind and spirit as well as the feet. In town, benches with backs are preferred. On grand loops the benches might be hand hewn by volunteers or could be flat rocks. In some spots there could also be picnic tables and other amenities such a shade structures, grills, or fire pits. Attractive and durable furnishings are available from commercial suppliers or could be built by in-house crews or volunteers.

Little Green Spots

On town walks, there are opportunities to create pleasant little landscaped spots. They are nooks with a small grassy area, a few shade trees, and a bench or two along a sidewalk. They can be a nice surprise along a route. Perhaps neighbors or local businesses can be encouraged to plant a few flowers there. They can be a nice touch, especially at intersections.

Commercial Amenities

This is not so much about building improvements as about laying out routes to access places to eat, drink, sleep, and get provisions. They should fit the rhythm of a hike or in-town walk. On a grand loop, these are shops, restaurants, or lodgings found in villages and hamlets or other spots. Because grand loops are close to cities, food trucks could join in as mobile service nodes to provide meals at key points along the routes. The feasibility of these services would be driven by market considerations such as whether there is enough hiker traffic at key points. It would be important to provide places or pads where these services could be set up, such as at trailheads or other convenient locations.

Because grand loops are often within mobile phone range as well as proximate to transit stops and affordable ride share services, people can travel light. With these conveniences, trekkers can return home or even back to a downtown hotel each night, returning to the trail the next morning. In theory, with points of mobile phone service available, a trekker could access almost any needed service at any trailhead.

Ready access to places at 10- to 12-mile intervals can facilitate traveling light, minimizing the need to carry a heavy backpack. Overnight needs can be met by hotels or B&Bs and publicly operated or commercial campgrounds that include tent, cabin, or yurt rentals. In town we consider the location of shops, restaurants, and hotels for both locals users and tourists.

Winter activities should be incorporated into projects where there is seasonal snow and ice. Considerations include availability of warming huts, ski and snowshoe rentals, and other cold weather support amenities. Setting tracks for Nordic skiing where appropriate to enable more users would be helpful too.

WAY STATIONS

This is a topic unique to grand loops, particularly where there may be significant expanses of open and stark open countryside, with no villages or amenities for miles. Spaces like these are found in the expansive ranchlands around Dallas–Ft. Worth, the marshy flatlands around cities in Florida, and in the deserts encircling Las Vegas and Phoenix.

Some routes may work seasonally but not in summer or winter. For most, these long expanses can be daunting, isolating, and threatening with heat, relentless sun, winds, storms, and even blizzards. Every attempt should be made to lay out routes that access settlements or other desirable places, but sometimes there are stark landscapes that must be traversed. Addressing these is a planning challenge but is not insurmountable.

Way stations—let's call them trail depots—can help address this challenge (figure 4.2). These are not service nodes per se, although some of these spots may offer amenities. They are appropriately spaced places of refuge and respite and en route destinations to mark the way and reward progress. They're inspired by the old-time stagecoach and railroad stops spaced to meet the needs of horses and drivers, service passengers, or provide water and coal for locomotives. In the case of the early day railroads, they were called water stops, placed maybe 7–10 miles apart.

Figure 4.2. Trail depot. (Credit: Bill Neumann)

On a grand loop, depots can be enclosed structures with benches, drinking water, toilets, and, where feasible, a cluster of trees for shade. Architectural features can be added to make the stops visible and appear reachable across the distances between them. At some locations there can be reservable huts, yurts, or other small structures for overnight accommodation. Arrangements can be made for services by food trucks or camping outfitters who come and set up camp. Ideally, these "oases," likened to old-time water stops, should be placed every 7 or 10 miles—a three- to four-hour walk. The designs can express cultural or ecological themes. They can be unifying and defining artifacts of a grand loop route. Some of these can be larger iconic features located at key junctures. Along these lines, Japan's Kumano Kodo has a 100-foot-tall feature, the Torii Arch, at Hongu, where trekkers begin or end their trail journeys.

Environmental Factors

These are the basic field conditions—the physical features of the corridor. They shape planning the best route to minimize impacts on the sensitive elements and minimizing the costs of negotiating difficult terrain. In many instances, some of these attributes, such as streams and ponds, shape the experience as well.

Always plan with the environment surrounding the trail or walkway in mind. Trails should be sited to avoid harming sensitive habitats, species, and historical and cultural sites and to protect unstable areas. Proactively plan to protect, enhance, and reveal (with interpretive displays) environmental, visual (both close-in and longer vistas), and culture features. Ideally, leave at least 150 feet (the width of three tree canopies) on either side of the trail centerline or as advised by ecology professionals. In the face of climate change, plan and design for resiliency.

This concept includes promoting proactive community engagement with opportunities for students, volunteers, youth, and seniors to participate in trail upkeep and environmental projects and preservation efforts.

Grades and Cross-Slopes

These affect construction costs, and, from a user perspective, they are a critical factor in addressing both comfort and abilities. Steep grades and cross-slopes can be a challenge both on grand loops and along town walks. Ideally, we want to avoid steep, long, and frequent ascents, generally keeping them less than 12 percent on grand loop trails and less than 5 percent on in-town walks. Cross-slopes of trails and walks should not exceed 2 percent to ensure a stable walking surface.

Terrain, Soils, and Drainage

Terrain, soils, and rain runoff form the primary underlying geological platform of a trail route. There is an essential interplay between trails, soils, and slopes, and we are concerned about the stability of underlying soils to support a stable trail surface and the potential for harmful erosion that improperly placed trails might cause. How prone is the soil under a trail tread to degrade and the trail surface to incise from heavy use? Trail corridor drainage and low spots can generally be revealed by looking at the terrain for hints about how rainwater will run off. What points are prone to erosion? Can we avoid creating low muddy spots that will not only impede users but promote excessive widening and braiding as people try to sidestep them? In many instances special structural features such as water bars to prevent erosion may be needed. In winter will there be hazardous icy spots? Will a trail route along a hillside scar the landscape, especially in a scenic area? Note that trail scars can really show when there is snow on the slope.

Water Features and Wetlands

Water features are critical. They include springs, creeks, waterfalls, canals, rivers, ponds, and shorelines. Consider the streams or water bodies themselves, and the riparian environments along their edges. The goal is to protect these sensitive areas and, where appropriate, to provide access to water features for viewing, drinking, fishing, and maybe taking a dip. These features are especially important because they are dynamic places that support life, replenish moisture, maintain water quality, sustain habitat for aquatic creatures including fish and other food sources to birds and animals, and provide a vital aesthetic resource for the trail experience. They are particularly sensitive to trail construction and use because they are vulnerable to disturbance such as filling, harmful sedimentation, and damage to shorelines, as well as disturbance of aquatic and other wild species that use these spaces.

Wetlands are vital and vulnerable areas of standing or slow-moving water that support plant and animal life, particularly phreatophytic (water-loving) species. Besides providing habitat, wetlands also clean water by filtering, store water, and regulate the speed and volume of runoff during storm events by capturing and holding water. Because they attract wildlife and showcase many attractive plant species, they are important areas of scenic and aesthetic interest to trail users. As very sensitive places, they are highly vulnerable to trail construction and use and can be damaged by filling or disturbance during maintenance operations. Wetlands are also strictly regulated under federal law and by state and local regulations. Permits may be required if there is encroachment.

Wildfires and Flooding

With climate change, wildfires have become a catastrophic issue. So too have violent storms and flash flooding. In other instances, such as during droughts, steams and springs may dry up, lessening the supply of drinking water along trails. From a grand loop trail perspective, this is a particular concern in what's called the wildland–urban interface. There is concern about hazards to trail users from these events. Land managers, adjacent property owners, and firefighters are also more vigilant about trail users potentially causing fires. Emergency evacuation and rescue are also factors. There are no simple answers to these questions, but where good information is available, there may be ways to avoid higher-risk areas. Several trail organizations including the Pacific Crest Trail Association have been carefully monitoring this growing concern and looking at steps to mitigate the issues.[5]

Contaminants: Water, Soil, and Air Quality

Water, soils, and air quality are considered from the perspective of both the trail user's experience and health and the impact of the trail on the environment. We want to avoid polluting places along a trail corridor while avoiding contaminated soils or water sources. Clean, fresh air is an important defining element of a good trail experience—not only to promote health and minimize unpleasant odors but also to avoid the impacts of smoke, smog, dust, and fumes. This includes both the local setting and long views out to the horizon. We want clean water for its aesthetic value but also for drinking or bathing in a stream, ocean, lake, or pond. We consider contaminants both from the user standpoint and from the potential adverse impacts on the environment, such as those of trail construction and maintenance.

Flora and Fauna

Gather information about the flora and fauna along routes. Trail construction, use, and maintenance can affect sensitive plants and animals by disturbing terrain, vegetation, and vulnerable areas along trails as well as the adjacent areas. Consider habitat, feeding and breeding areas, and routes of movement and migration. Trail activities can also adversely affect native vegetation. Always pursue best preservation practices, particularly with respect to threatened and endangered species, and ensure conformance with federal, state, and local regulations.

Weeds and Pests

Trail construction and use can introduce weeds and other invasive species (both plant and animal pests). This can significantly harm the ecological integrity of an area. Invasive species such as weeds and certain destructive land animals, insects, birds, and aquatic creatures can crowd out native species, reduce diversity, and disrupt the ecological balance and integrity in multiple ways. Invasives such as the pine beetle can destroy broad swaths of forest and thereby increase hazards of fire, erosion, and stream sedimentation, among other problems. Think about how to best plan, develop, and manage trails to minimize harm and, where needed, mitigate the effects of invasive species.

Unauthorized Trails

The physical features of a site such as terrain can also influence patterns of travel. In laying out routes, try to anticipate where social (unauthorized) trails might be created and try aligning routes to discourage them. This is growing problem with the increased popularity of trails when users leave the established trail and take their own unauthorized routes, such as cutting across switchbacks. In town it might be cutting across a lawn. Repeated violations of this sort create scars, damage vegetation, promote erosion, increase maintenance and enforcement costs, disturb nearby residents, and otherwise result in serious management problems.

Effective trail planning and policymaking must address this problem to prevent, preempt, and repair areas that have been damaged. In some cases, social trails reflect a flaw in the initial trail design and layout, and users are "designing" a more functional route with their feet. Unauthorized trails should be assessed to determine whether the social trail or some variation might be a better route.

Access, Continuity, Connectivity, Accessibility, and Linkage Opportunities

People should be able to conveniently reach a trail and, once there, be able to travel the corridor without impediments. Connectivity is the degree to which the trail is integrated with its surroundings, including communities, neighborhoods, and commercial areas as well as with local trails and sidewalk networks. Accessibility is the degree to which the trail can be used by people with a wide range of abilities, including people with disabilities as defined by the Americans with Disabilities Act (ADA) and similar legislation in other countries.

Points of Access

In planning a route this involves noting suitable places for trailheads both for drive-up and walk-up facilities.

Drive-up trailhead sites should have room for parking and other entry amenities such as shelters, toilets, and drinking water. Drive-up sites typically include places to park, a signed gateway point, and ideally a shelter. Toilets and drinking water facilities are essential. Facilities must accommodate people with disabilities. A prominent, easy-to-read trail map or wayfinding display is a must, showing the route, terrain, distances, degree of difficulty, and other information to guide visitors. The site should be attractively designed and buffered from neighboring properties. A gate may be desirable to prevent unauthorized after-hours parking. Overflow should also be addressed to avoid cars parking on roadways in nearby neighborhoods or otherwise creating a nuisance.

Walk-up entry points are more applicable to town walks (figure 4.3) and are more typical for people arriving on foot, on bikes, or by transit. They are simpler and don't take as much space. They should be visible, attractive, and compatible with the surrounding neighborhoods. There can be an architectural gateway element announcing and celebrating the pathway and a small display and a map with a "you are here" marker, showing the location of amenities such rest spots, drinking water and toilets, convenience stores, and other useful information. Where appropriate there could be benches, drinking water, and perhaps a toilet facility.

Figure 4.3. Walk-up trailhead. (Credit: Bill Neumann)

In both cases they should be situated to not adversely impact surrounding properties. All access points should be convenient and visible from the road or street system. Sites should be located and designed to facilitate public transit and rideshare access. Working with transit agencies to provide stops at trail entry points and to note them on route maps is helpful. Also be sure to enable rideshare service dropoff and pickup at access points. Check to see whether cellular service is available. If not, perhaps a call box can be installed, useful for both hailing a ride and calling in an emergency.

Note that in some jurisdictions, overcrowding of trailhead parking areas has become a significant problem, with cars spilling out into surrounding areas and users being turned away. To address this problem, some places have set up transit shuttles to trailheads. The City of Boulder, Colorado, Open Space Department provides this alternative to driving, for example. Hikers can be dropped off at one trailhead, hike along a trail, and be picked up at another.

In planning trailheads, note that they are sometimes locations for criminal activity, so visibility and surveillance must be factored in. Good routine maintenance and patrol of trailheads are helpful.

Continuity

To be functional and desirable, the route must be designed so that users can travel the whole way without impediments or difficult or uncomfortable segments. In the initial phases of development, the route may or may not satisfy all these goals, but at least it should be logical, with no dead ends or unsafe, unsavory areas.

Connectivity and Wayfinding

Connectivity is about the trail or walk linking to meaningful destinations, points of interest, service nodes to get provisions, and other trails. It's also about walkable connections to nearby residential areas and places of work. Grand loops should connect regional parks, open spaces, existing trails, and other outdoor features. Town walks should link neighborhoods, parks, schools, shopping, greenways, and other important civic destinations. Consider promoting open space and nature connectivity by creating green corridors between existing large, preserved parcels. Consider the longer-range creation of integrated networks linking grand loops and town walks as well as connecting to longer-distance trails that might pass near the area.

Wayfinding is critical both to enjoy a trek and for safety reasons, to avoid getting lost and being able to report your location in an emergency. An easy-to-follow system should be installed in the field with clear, tasteful markers. There should be concise messaging without sign clutter. Comprehensive overview information should be posted at trailheads and other entry points. It should also promote a sense of place and present identity branding that defines and promotes the trail or walkway as a special, high-quality route. Wayfinding elements include maps, mile markers, and directional arrows. Mile markers and directional arrows offer comfort and reassurance. They should be at half-mile intervals and, importantly, at any decision point such as a trail intersection. A marker can be a stamp in the pavement, a post, or a sculptural element. At the rudimentary level it might be a simple blaze on a tree or post or a painted stripe on the sidewalk, as along Tucson's Turquoise Trails. Korea's Jeju Olle has a small metal horse sculpture with the head pointing the way. For most trails, physical markers are preferable to printed maps or digital guides because there is not always reliable cell service, and printed guides may be hard to come by.

LEGAL SIGNS

These include regulatory and safety signage. They're particularly necessary where other modes of travel are present, such as bikes or automobiles. Most of these signs must conform to the specific graphic, size, and placement standards. There are official guidelines such as the US Manual of Uniform Traffic Control Devices.

INTERPRETIVE DISPLAYS, ARTS AND CRAFTS

These range from a simple podium-style display to a sculptural element. Several companies produce durable, attractive displays, and artists can produce sculptures, murals, or other art. Artifacts such as a farm implement can be mounted as interpretive displays. There may be opportunities to encourage musicians, dancers, and poets. To accommodate these performances, consider creating performing pads or mini-amphitheaters. There can also be opportunities for scheduled exhibits, art shows, and craft displays. Durability and vandal resistance are always key considerations.

Accessibility

Trails and walking routes should be visible, readily accessible, and enjoyable for a full range of user demographics, ethnicities, income levels, age groups, genders, and abilities. The routes should also be family and kid friendly. This implies surfaces, grades, and routes that are that are generally walkable, with no special abilities or heavy backpack required.

In thinking about planning a route, it is essential to consider the different levels of challenges to potential users, from people with joint problems to those needing mobility devices such as wheelchairs. This is important both in providing access and enjoyment for as many people as possible and in meeting legal requirements such as those spelled out in the ADA.

According to census data and other sources, more than 3 million people in the United States need wheelchairs for mobility.[6] Add in people who rely on other mobility devices such as walkers, canes, and crutches and the number increases to over 6 million.[7] With people who use hiking poles or walking sticks, the number grows, although these people may have more flexibility in the types of trails surfaces and terrains they can comfortably negotiate. Taking all these needs into account, there are a lot of people who face physical challenges, many of whom want to use trails and walks to expand their access to outdoor places.

There are complexities in planning and designing to include more users with disabilities, but increasingly, there are solutions. In addition to infrastructure elements such as a level, firm surface, slopes that do not exceed wheelchair-negotiable grades, curb ramps, and adequate width for two wheelchairs to pass, there are evolving technologies such as specialized all-terrain wheelchairs and walkers that enable negotiating more challenging terrain. Staunton State Park in Colorado has an inventory of highly mobile Track Chairs and has a network of natural-appearing but properly graded trails.[8] Minnesota has a similar program. Interestingly, the trail surface texture and cross-section shown in the Staunton State Park Accessibility Brochure match the optimal proposed grand loop trail design.

The accessibility challenge is more formidable in planning the more varied surfaces of grand loops. In some instances, there may be opportunities to provide parallel, more negotiable alternative routes that bypass the more challenging sections of terrain.

Accessibility includes having a range of hiking or walking distance options. There should be strategically placed close-in points of access by transit and affordable rideshare transportation. Access should be a short, easy trip from all residents: less than an hour to a grand loop trailhead and, ultimately, a ten-minute walk (half a mile) from doorsteps for town walks.

For mobility-challenged such as those who use wheelchairs and for others who have vision, hearing, or cognitive disabilities, the question of accessibility is more difficult, especially when natural surface trails are built through more rugged terrain. Ideally, we want to have entire systems that meet universal accessibility standards, such as having a smooth, level, 5-foot-wide tread and grades of 8.3 percent or less throughout, but achieving this, especially on grand loops, is unlikely. The cost, environmental impacts, and the desire to have a more backcountry experience make this impractical. Town walks, on the other hand, typically follow routes that have paved treads, curb ramps, and other improvements that can conform to legislation such as the ADA,

although there are still many places with narrow walks or other impediments. In some cities, such as San Francisco, there is inherently challenging terrain that presents formidable challenges. That said, there may
be ways to mitigate. For example, along a grand loop, consider offering
more accommodating alternative routes where users can bypass more
difficult sections. New accessibility technologies are being developed,
including wheeled backcountry trekking devices such as the multiter-
rain vehicles developed by innovators such as Peter Axelson of Beneficial Design.

Opportunities to String Together Existing Routes

When laying out a route, check to see what existing trails, walks, or
other usable segments are already there or nearby. Note also where
existing parks, open space preserves, and other green places are and
consider how they could be woven together into a grand loop or town
walk. In drafting the Denver Grand Loop Concept Plan, for example,
there was already significant mileage of existing trails running along the
edges of the city. In that instance, it became an exercise of connecting
pieces together rather than building a whole new course. Connecting
the dots gave the concept an added appeal to the open space agencies
along the proposed route. Similarly, the Maricopa Trail had significant
existing segments, particularly along the existing irrigation canal maintenance paths.

Land Use and Cultural Context

"Human-scape" features such as history and culture offer opportunities
for interpretive displays along a trail or walk. There are also questions of
public sensitivities and legal restrictions to be considered in protecting
these assets.

Ownership and Development Factors

Property ownership, rights of way, and developmental factors are critical, including the regulatory context of the area. This can be a particularly sensitive area. In the case of a grand loop project, we should look for strategically located public properties, such as state parks or open spaces, that can be featured and strategically tied together. When looking at parcel maps, strive to avoid clusters of small lots that are harder to traverse when securing rights of way. Examine the road networks to determine routing potentials in dedicated rights of way along the edges of roads and potential walkable streets where there are low traffic volumes and speeds. In some instances, existing and proposed utility corridors can be potential routes, but consider aesthetics as part of that option. Utility ways can be straight and monotonous and humming; crackling wires and rows of towers are not a great experience. For town walks it's important to know about any planned projects, including street widenings, sidewalk improvements, and neighborhood redevelopment activities.

Finally, we want to understand the land use planning context, including urbanization patterns, permitted types of land uses, and the likelihood of future development, including commercial and industrial projects. In this investigation, consider the regulatory framework that might offer opportunities for securing dedicated rights of way when properties develop. We also want to know of any planned or likely projects such as a proposed mining or logging operation, an airport expansion, or other activity that might block a corridor. Consulting with the local jurisdiction planning entities along routes can help with this information. There is additional discussion of rights of way in chapter 5.

Nearby Properties and Activities

Will the trail or walk potentially disturb nearby residents, businesses, or agricultural activities or create the perception that they will be disturbed?

Are there ways to buffer these uses to reduce conflicts? Consider how the trail or walk will affect motorists to avoid conflicts, both where there are on-road segments and at intersections. Respect property rights and be a good neighbor by avoiding disruption or disturbance or compromising privacy. Trails and walking routes should not create nuisances.

Cultural Values

These can include historic sites and structures, tribal sites, artifacts, archeological features, paleontological sites, and contemporary features such as ethnic characteristics or neighborhood character. Trail construction and use can potentially disturb sites, structures, and neighborhood character. Trails and walks can adversely alter landscapes, bring in outsiders, promote undesired development, and have other impacts, sometimes very subtle, on local communities. On the positive side, trail routes offer opportunities for visitors to learn about history and local culture through interpretation and experience when passing through locales of historic, cultural, or ethnic interest. In addition, routing a trail or walk through such areas may bring economic and pride benefits when the local inhabitants want to showcase these features, such as with restaurants or craft shops. Note that there may be regulatory compliance requirements, including documentation, protection, and mitigation.

Interpretation and Educational Opportunities

Consider opportunities to interpret, educate, extoll health benefits, expand awareness, and promote an ethic of stewardship. Featuring these elements enriches a trail experience and can promote caring for its environmental setting. Identify places for interpretive displays and consider how routing can be aligned to access points of interest. Perhaps schools can use the trail or walk as an outdoor classroom. Think about potentials for volunteer trail building and environmental stewardship projects.

Management Considerations

Once a project is built, someone must take care of it. Sometimes maintenance is overlooked in the planning process, yet it is all important, especially if the trail or walk is to be well received by the entity that will manage it. This section lays out what grand loop and town walk management entails.

Good management starts with good planning. This is how we avoid unnecessary costs and burdens later on. Solid management also promotes a high-quality experience, protecting the surrounding environment and user safety and security. Management includes maintaining facilities, patrol and rescue, special events, and other activities and requirements. Addressing long-term planning and resource stewardship is also important. There are multiple components to consider, including soft-surface trails; paved sidewalks and trails, streets, and roads where walking is integrated into the street or road system; and associated amenities such as rest areas, landscaped areas, miniparks, features, open spaces, viewsheds, woodlots, streams, and wetlands, as well as cultural and interpretive elements. Management should consider not only the trail itself but also the associated corridors. These can be 20 feet wide or more depending on the setting, the ecology, and the other resources involved.

Maintenance

Maintenance includes routine day-to-day tasks such as sweeping and minor repairs and longer-term remedial functions such as replacing a pedestrian bridge or rebuilding a retaining wall. There are also seasonal functions, including removing ice and snow or managing peak season crowds. We want durable, sustainable trails and walkways that can endure with minimal upkeep and replacement costs. They should be state-of-the-art designs, affordable to build and maintain. Consider costs and budgets and the feasibility of raising maintenance funds. Pursue partnerships with other agencies where trails can also serve as flood control, utility maintenance, or wildfire mitigation access routes. Good management begins with durable components and an effective, adequately funded management organization in place. To underpin this effort, community groups, residents, business owners, developers, and other stakeholders should be engaged, with timely response to reported concerns. There should be best management practices and a consistent standard of care and quality across multiple jurisdictional boundaries.

Regular inspection is a must, with designated personnel regularly walking the corridors and documenting and reporting problems. There should be protocols and capacity for prompt follow-up to address problems. This is particularly important with it comes to potential hazards and liability risks. In the face of climate change, this includes wildfire risk monitoring of conditions such as drought, burnable fuel buildup, and coordination with firefighters to immediately respond to a fire incident. The following is a checklist of key operations and maintenance items:

- Trail and walking surface repair
- Litter and trash removal and graffiti cleanup
- Fixtures and furnishings such as rest areas, benches, toilets, and drinking water facilities
- "Social trails" and shortcuts
- Paved trail and sidewalk sweeping
- Street sweeping and snow and ice removal
- Lighting, striping, and traffic signal maintenance

- On-street surfaces: pavement, signage, striping, and delineators
- Snow and ice removal as appropriate (paved trails)
- Natural resource stewardship and enhancement
- Signage and wayfinding devices
- Vandalism repair
- Erosion control
- Vegetation management, including weeding, tree trimming including ensuring head clearance, and fallen tree removal
- Landscape management such as medians and grassy areas, including irrigation
- Pests and invasive species
- Programming and events
- Waterfowl and hunting regulation and conflict management, if applicable
- Patrol, law enforcement, and rescue

Carrying Capacity and Crowding

With the increasing popularity of trails and other outdoor activities, in many places there is a growing challenge in dealing with more people arriving than the site can handle. This affects trail facilities and resources and degrades the experience. There are no simple answers, but it is important to consider the anticipated user numbers and think about ways to reduce adverse impacts. Building grand loops and town walks can help by offering more miles of trails and walking routes to accommodate users. On the other hand, because they are readily accessible, they could attract many more visitors. Planners should anticipate ways to spread out users, maybe harden some areas with more durable surfaces such as compacted gravel, and consider side loops off the main trail to accommodate more people. It is also important to consider the impact of special events such as races or organized group hikes and recommend management provisions to ensure that they don't overwhelm the system or adversely affect the enjoyment by regular users.

Safety, Security, Risk, and Liability Considerations

Consider both safety and the perception of safety. There are multiple challenges, including injuries, assaults, thefts, unstable slopes, lightning, heavy rain, flash floods, rocks and tree branches that could fall, fires, lost hikers, and many other unanticipated contingencies. Personal security from crime is important. Coupled with this is the question of emergency access, rescue and evacuation, and communications between emergency personnel. A risk management approach proactively seeks to minimize problems. That means anticipating hazards and planning and designing to avoid them, such as by stabilizing slopes, providing hand railings where needed, and considering good lines of sight, to mention a few. It is important to consult with land managers, police, and fire and rescue professionals during the planning process and, of course, with design professionals. Get input from stakeholders of different genders, ethnicities, and age groups early in the process. Comply with established published guidelines and standards to promote safety and reduce liability exposure.

We now move on to the nuts and bolts: planning guidance and components that can be used to carve out rights of way.

CHAPTER 5

Laying Out a Route

"Don't fight nature. Try to see the trail in the landscape."

—Chuck Flink, author of *The Greenway Imperative*[1]

Overcoming barriers and laying out a route is about assembling resources, solving problems, and making deals. It can be daunting. Having an inspiring, workable plan and support people in place helps. So does the ability to adjust, improvise, and adapt and not be discouraged. Sometimes you need to find a workaround, and flexibility is essential.

In years of doing this, I've found encouragement from a set of precepts. Let's call them the four Ps: patience, preparedness, politeness, and persistence.

- **Patience.** Before even starting, recognize that laying out routes and securing rights of way and approvals takes time, in some cases months, even years. Clearly you want to move as expeditiously as you can, but you also need to be realistic and be sure your project sponsors or clients understand that it takes time. Conveying that message upfront is important to keep credibility. However, reassure people that it's a great plan, and steps like securing rights of way and permits are part of the process. It takes time, but you'll get it done.

- **Preparedness.** Find out in advance what properties or permissions you will need and who the key contacts and decision makers are. Assemble the people with the skills to negotiate, communicate, draw up legal agreements, or prepare design modifications. Be sure the agency that will take ownership and manage the properties and improvements is on board. Resources with guidance on successful tactics include the Trust for Public Land (TPL), the Rails-to-Trails Conservancy, and American Trails. There are similar master plans by others and how-to books available as well. (See *Helpful Resources* at end of this book.) Some entities such as the TPL can provide hands-on assistance.
- **Politeness.** Listen to and work with all the players, even the most gnarly ones. Diplomacy is everything! Most reasonable things are negotiable. Be ready to deal, and at the same time know what are your positions of strength and who your influential allies are.
- **Persistence (ask six times).** In negotiating with property owners or agency decision makers, I've often heard this sequence: "Hell no and don't call me again," "Nope, can't do it," "Its' impossible!" "Show me how that can be done," "Uh maybe," and "Okay." I call this process the "ask six times" strategy. Once, while attempting to create a path adjacent to a mainline railroad, we ran into a dead end. I contacted the railroad right-of-way people for months but got no reply. When I finally did make contact, I was told, "Forget it." After more than a year I became discouraged and told the city public works director who was my client that we were probably at the end of our rope. A few weeks later he called and said, "You know, I own a couple shares in the holding company that owns the railroad. Maybe I'll just go

to the shareholders' meeting." I thought he was joking. A few weeks later he called and said, "The vice president of the railroad wants to meet you and see the project." Sure enough, at the shareholder's meeting my client had buttonholed the guy and made his pitch. "This is really cool," the VP said as we looked over the trail site. "Send me your drawings and a letter and we'll get this done." And that was that. Thousands now enjoy that "impossible" trail.

Carving Out Rights of Way

An effective rights-of-way acquisition strategy includes several tactics that can make the process easier and result in better outcomes.

Start by Thinking Big, Best, and Out of the Box

You can always scale back and compromise, if need be, but it's hard to go back and ask for something you did not initially propose. Another part of this mindset when you encounter any potential obstruction is to think "over, under, around, or through." Is there any way to get around an obstruction?

Grab the Low-Hanging Fruit

From the plan map and spreadsheet there should be a clear picture of the easy-to-acquire segments. These potentially include existing trails that can be connected, large public park and open space holdings where managers are open to the trail passing through, floodplains and other minimally developable areas, and of course existing walkable local streets, back roads, and sidewalks. Be sure the appropriate agency managers and engineers are consulted.

Note the Large Parcels and Avoid Small Lots

The street grid shown on the base maps, aided by satellite views on a service such as Google Maps, should give you a rough idea of the wider open areas and the built-up areas. Try to string your way along, linking routes through or along the edge of big parcels rather than having to deal with potentially hundreds of small lots. Later on you can pull out actual parcel maps from the assessor's office, but for now the blank spaces and the green spaces should give you a general idea.

Consider and Plot Alternative Routes

Be ready to address contingencies. Include a backup plan on your right-of-way reconnaissance map. This means considering and plotting alternative routes as needed in places to bypass or otherwise work around what you anticipate might be difficult areas. Be sure the second and maybe third choices still offer a high-quality, safe option.

Look for Joint Use of Corridors

In building the Metro Denver Greenway network, the Denver Urban Drainage and Flood Control District was a great partner in securing trail rights of way. For the greenway advocates it was a trail project. For the Flood Control District, it was a floodway maintenance access road. It was a win–win, and no one has more clout than a well-funded flood protection agency. The same potential exists along irrigation canals. The Maricopa Trail in around Phoenix follows canal access roads.

Rail lines have potential out-of-service routes and trails with rails where a trail is incorporated into an active train route. The Rails-to-Trails Conservancy has all kinds of resources and professional advice on this topic. Utility corridors such gas, sewer, and overhead electrical lines have potential, although in many instances these do not include surface trail rights and they are not always the most aesthetically pleasing settings. For in-town routes there may be opportunities to share rights of way with transit tracks. This strategy provides a section of a walking loop trail and creates the potential to combine walking segments with the option of hopping on the transit train if tired.

With climate change, there is increasing need for wildfire fighting access roads. This presents another joint use opportunity on grand loops, particularly in wildland–urban interface areas. Although there may be some concern that trail users could cause fires, the other side of the coin is that hikers might be the ones to first spot and report a fire. Town walks can be emergency evacuation routes during floods, terrorist attacks, or other events.

Look at the Regulatory and Developer Incentive Process

For decades trails, open space, and land conservation elements have been incorporated into subdivision approvals. Many developers have done this voluntarily because market studies show that trails and walks are an essential home sales component. To encourage less motivated developers, communities have written trail dedication provisions into their codes. Sometimes these involve dedicating the right of way and building the trail. In other instances, cash in lieu is paid so a jurisdiction can acquire rights of way at more opportune locations. Other trades and incentives such as density bonuses work by allowing the developer to sell more units in return for dedicating a right of way. In this approach, proposed trails should be part of an adopted comprehensive plan, and these trails must be opened to the public, not restricted to residents.[2]

Check into Capital Improvement Plans

Although increasingly pedestrian uses are being incorporated into agency plans and programs, it's not always the case. A good starting point when contemplating a route is to gather transportation plans and scheduled improvements and confer with officials and engineers to be sure high-quality trails or walking routes are incorporated into designs and budgets. Having plans in place that show priority routes and the desired cross-sections would be a big help. It's also a good idea to line up allies among elected officials,

Look for Walkable and Adaptable Roads

Where rights of way for off-road trails or walks are readily available, look for walkable roads that could form connections. Some of these may be fine as is. Others may need improvements to make them suitable. Again, check existing plans and scheduled improvement programs and confer with the agency engineers. When it comes to working with traffic engineers, Elizabeth Stolfus, a seasoned transportation and traffic engineering consultant I interviewed, recommends being clear and discerning in your language. "Convey that your concept is distinct, so it's not stereotyped." She recommends, "When you say 'trail' or 'path' many picture a 'multi-use path,' a well-defined industry design component, typically a paved hike/bike trail, and that is limiting." She adds, "Everybody cares about safety! Safety counts. It's the foundation for other benefits and that's how to approach officials."[3]

Prepare Consistent, Nonthreatening Messaging

Good communication and messaging are at the core of successful right-of-way and approval negotiations. Following are a few key tips.

Keep the First Go-Round Completely Internal

During the initial planning and right-of-way strategizing it's important not to publicize details on acquisition or to publish any maps with lines on them—not on social media, not on a website, not anywhere! The last thing you want is an angry landowner or perturbed city engineer asking whether you're planning to take their property or mess around with their streets. Surprises like these are not good. There are ways to more productively engage these folks later in the process. At you begin to go public it's essential to have a simple, concise, clear, nonthreatening message about the project that overviews the idea, a few of the benefits, and a reassurance that the rights and input of property owners and managers will be respected and incorporated into the process.

Be aware that not too far along in the initial discussion phase there will be public meetings, with maps and plan documents presented. Be very careful about how initial maps are laid out. Rest assured that property owners will show up at meetings, and some will walk in already hostile. My colleagues and I have seen property owner see a marker line on the map that appears to go through their property and be very unhappy, including threatening to sue or worse. Some have even seen the not-to-scale line that, in the real world, would be a quarter mile wide and assume that we want to take a quarter-mile-wide swath from them. So, during this initial conceptual phase, make the lines on the maps informal, post disclaimers clarifying that the actual locations and widths are not yet determined, and remind attendees that you plan to speak directly with any potentially affected landowners.

Work One to One and Don't Threaten People

Although you're not publicizing the right-of-way plans, you do want to identify and reach out individually to each potentially affected party. It's not a good idea to surprise property owners or agency managers. Do some homework so you know something about their concerns and aspirations and begin to reach out to them informally. Also begin to assemble a list of things you might have to offer them. This process should be respectful and built around equitable, mutually beneficial transactions. Think about what's in it for them. Know that there's a good chance they will tell their neighbors, so tread very carefully and be prepared for possible irate emails and phone calls. It should never be a zero-sum game. Even if the owner is ornery, or even threatening, try to see their side and figure out what they want. Also, don't assume it's just about the money. I've learned there is often something deeper. Sometimes it's just wanting to be respected and appreciated—or simply saving face. Maybe you can arrange a trade, such as improving the road to their property or repairing the streetlights.

Finally, avoid eminent domain (condemnation) at all costs. That process is long and painful, and word will spread very quickly down the line if any property owner feels threatened by "the government taking their land." This approach is not likely to end well!

Have a Well-Informed, Competent Designated Spokesperson

This is usually the project leader with both communication and diplomatic skills. This person needs to be tactful, patient, and polite but persistent. Others on the team should not be making public statements or negotiating without first clearing with the designated leader or spokesperson.

Negotiate

This is where the rubber meets the road. I've often done the trail negotiation work successfully myself. If you're not comfortable with that approach, there are professional right-of-way negotiators who secure pipeline or highway rights of way and are experienced in this kind of work. Many cities and counties have real estate negotiators on staff.

The key is going into a negotiation with a basic understanding of the legalities but, more importantly, having lined up what you have to trade. Sometimes there's an engineering question involved to fit the trail into the site or a need to solve another problem an owner is concerned about. Can you find a workaround to address any of their needs? For example, on a trail project near Denver, to get permission to build a trail behind a woman's antique shop we agreed to build a sidewalk in front of her shop. With similar trades and tweaks, we've negotiated rights of way through a water treatment plant, next to an oil refinery, and through a working gravel mine, with the trail passing under a conveyor belt. Typically, the first meeting is about hearing what the owner wants then going back to put together a solution.

Prepare the Conveyance Instruments

There are several legal instruments by which rights of way are conveyed. The one you choose depends on which best suits the situation and the preferences of the parties. Here is an overview of the overview of the more common ones.

FEE SIMPLE

This grantor conveys full ownership of the property, granting a deed and relinquishing all previously held rights in the property. Typically, this is the most expensive way to go and can be problematic because this type of agreement may take away all uses such as a residence or business unless there is a leaseback agreement. Fee simple is almost never needed to build trails.

EASEMENTS

This is a grant of an overlying right that typically does not interfere (or if so, minimally) with the owner's use and enjoyment of their land. Ideally the easement is wide enough to accommodate both the trail and a buffer zone for landscaping, shade trees, and other trail-related elements. If possible, the conveyance includes a conservation component preserving ecological or other site values. This is the optimal kind of right of way to secure and much less costly. Sometimes landowners grant an easement in return for tax benefits or improvements to their property.

LICENSES, PERMITS, AND REVOKABLE PERMITS

These are not grants of real property like a fee simple conveyance or an easement. They are a permission. Typically, we see these when building on public property and infrastructure such as a highway right of way or along a railroad or utility corridor. It's often the necessary tool in these instances, although one of downsides is that they might be modified or eventually revoked at the will of the grantor. The permanence of the agreement depends on the language in the conveyance instrument. When securing rights of way like these, it's a good idea to have a "plan B" alternative route in case the permit is revoked.

PRESCRIPTIVE EASEMENTS AND ADVERSE POSSESSION

In this scenario, if people use a route continuously over a period of years without objection or obstruction by the landowner, a de facto right of way exists. This is a rare situation, and in litigation the landowner may prevail.

OPTIONS, FIRST REFUSAL, LEASE PURCHASE, AND LAND INSTALLMENT CONTRACT

There are other forms of conveyance that are useful in certain circumstances, including options to buy, a right of first refusal where the owner agrees to come to you first before selling the land or accepting a payment to hold the property for you. These can be ways to hold on to a potential right of way while you secure the resources to acquire it. Lease purchase is a related tool where you rent the right of way, build the trail, and agree to a later full conveyance. If the agreement specifies it, rent payments might count toward the ultimate full ownership. Land installment contracts are a similar method where rather than rent, the acquisition is paid off in regular installments until the full price is met and the deed is transferred.

THIRD-PARTY OWNERSHIP

In some instances, the right of way can be held by a third party such as a land trust or nonprofit association. This might be useful when a landowner doesn't want to convey property to the government. A private entity holding the conveyance might be acceptable. There are other instances where a public agency is not willing or unable to hold and manage property.

Close the Deal

Once the needed rights of way have been identified and the owners initially contacted, there is the process of preparing the conveyance agreement. This starts with an attorney with real estate expertise drafting the document. These documents are usually not highly complex, and templates can be found in public records of similar conveyances in the jurisdiction where the agreement will be executed.

Part of this step is due diligence and compliance, ensuring that there are no problematic environmental issues such as contaminants on the site or other constraints to building a trail such as historic artifacts or sensitive wildlife. If any of these are found, then there needs to be a plan to mitigate impacts to the satisfaction of the appropriate reviewing authorities such as wildlife, environmental protection, historic, and cultural officials. In many cases solutions can be found. Finally, it needs to be clear who the legal grantee will be who accepts the property, who will be responsible for operations and maintenance, and how upkeep will be funded.

Liability and Recreational Use Statutes

In wrapping up the right-of-way discussion, it is important to address liability concerns. In an increasingly litigious society, risks of personal injury need to be addressed. With climate change, the potential for damages associated with catastrophic fires makes things even more complex. In procuring easements, licenses, permits, and other grants of right of way, realize that the grantor may rightfully be concerned about their exposure to lawsuits and liability insurance impacts from a trail on or near their property.

To address such concerns, all fifty US states have passed recreational use statutes (RUSs). This is a mechanism whereby the government has taken significant steps to insulate landowners from liability when they grant free recreational access such as easements for trails. Although the risks of litigation with RUSs in place have been very low, the liability still remains a concern among landowners. Indeed, although RUS protections significantly limit liability, they do not fully prevent a lawsuit by an aggrieved trail user. For example, protections do not apply to "willful, wanton, or malicious" failure to warn or guard against a dangerous condition. And there have been rare cases against landowners who have granted rights of way. Fortunately, many government entities have immunity or limits on liability when they accept easements for trails.[4] Some states, such as Florida, have specified limits of liability for private property owners whose lands are along routes designated as part of the statewide trail system.[5]

Buffering

Along significant segments of many trails and walks, the surroundings are less pleasant, and there is a need to create a backdrop along the edges of the corridor that uses landscaping, grading, screen walls, art, or other features to create a pleasant walking space. This is called buffering.

Many of us who plan trails tend to first picture the place as viewed from 10,000 feet above. If the trail goes through a vast forest or open space on a map, we get an impression of a wild area, away from it all. We want grand vistas, primeval forests, and verdant meadows all along the way, but those expectations can be limiting, especially for closer-in routes near or in cities. Most urban areas don't have vast open spaces, but there are places where you can create the perception of being in nature, especially with buffered edges. In many cases, to accomplish the perception of pleasant surroundings, the corridor may need be only a hundred feet wide or less. If the edges are properly designed with trees, grading, or other filtering, harsher surroundings can be screened out, leaving a sense of being in greener place.

This concept of buffering has particularly rung true for me laying out greenway corridors along rivers and streams. Many times, we would first scout a greenway route by paddling a canoe or kayak along an urban watercourse. Viewing from above on a map, you'd expect a cacophony of repelling factors, but when on the river itself, the sloping banks and the adjacent wooded riparian almost totally screens them. The Wolf River Greenway in Memphis winds through some of the city's roughest edges, with industries, highways, railroads, dirt bike tracks, and dumps. Yet in many places you'd think you were somewhere in the great north woods. The harsh sights are not visible, and the city sounds are only a din in the background.

The key is to have a pleasant core space from the point of view of the person on the pathway, and adequate buffering can make it work. Think of it as an experiential bubble (figure 5.1). This is the frame of perception. It consists of a hierarchy of concentric spaces: the intimate, nearby, midrange, and distant perspectives.

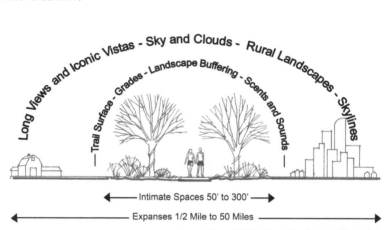

Figure 5.1. The experiential bubble. (Credit: Bill Neumann)

As you scout your routes, consider these bubbles and think about ways to optimize the core space first by choosing existing buffered routes. Where these are not available, use design solutions such as landscaping, other screening, and other aesthetic treatments to make the experience in the bubble appealing.

Buffering is an important consideration when planning treads and corridors, as is avoiding adverse impacts on adjacent properties and ecologically sensitive areas.

Types of Treads and Corridors

With the flexibility of foot travel, we can envision eight primary types of treads and corridors. Note that in applying each, design details such as landscaping, traffic devices, retaining walls, stabilization, drainage, fencing, and hand railings must be factored in and local regulations considered.[6,7]

Natural Surface Trails

These will probably make up significant portions of a grand loop trail. Ideally the route goes through undeveloped regions with attractive open landscapes (figure 5.2). Portions might pass through a state park or forest preserve or along a shoreline. Widths may vary, although a 4- to 6-foot width is preferred, with a buffered edge. In some instances, where confined by terrain, the trail may be narrower and more primitive.

Figure 5.2. Natural surface trail. (Credit: Bill Neumann)

Paved Shared-Use Pathways

These are usually in more built-up settings and used if a paved hike/bike path is desired, such as in the Las Vegas and Louisville grand loops. Even in the case of a predominantly walking route, this type may be used if there are opportunities to follow existing hike/bike trails through neighborhoods along the way. Typically, they are concrete or asphalt, although the surface might be crushed and compacted gravel fines. If bikes are present, the tread should be a minimum of 10 feet wide. They should have with longer lines of sight than walking paths and grades typically less than 5 percent. They require more substantial infrastructure, such as pedestrian bridges, retaining walls, and railings.[8] Ideally, if a shared-use trail segment is needed, there is a separate parallel walking path.

Think Flexible Treads

For most present-day hike/bike paths, the rate-determining design factor is the skinny tire road bike. As for streets, roads, and highways, there are strict guidelines for trail width, surface, sight lines, and other factors. We can think differently when planning many grand loops and town walks. We can picture them as human-powered ATV routes. That's because humans, or for that matter, horses, are mechanically built to tread on nearly any surface. Similarly, the mountain bike is the all-terrain version of a street bike. Although grand loops and town walks have their challenges, there is more freedom in the ways you can design them. A single route need not have a single type of tread. There can be an array of cross-sections with multiple types of treads, surfaces, and dimensions.

The Maricopa Trail is a good example of this flexible mix. According to R. J. Cardin, Maricopa County parks director, the predominant cross-section is a 4-foot-wide earthen trail, but the route also includes paved paths, streets, and sidewalks, depending on local conditions.[9] Note that the *2014 Maricopa Country Regional Trail System Plan*, available online, can be a useful "design manual" for details of how to lay out a 300-plus-mile trail with a mix of trail types and trail corridor treatments.[10] Denver's 5280 Trail also has a variety of cross-sections. A useful design manual for that project can also be found online with a full package of details and advice.[11]

Separated Treads

This is a useful concept for a trail corridor that serves both foot travel and bicycle use. In some instances, particularly along a grand loop, it is desirable to buffer one pathway use with spatial and visual separation (figure 5.3).

Figure 5.3. Separated trail. (Credit: Bill Neumann)

High-Quality Sidewalks

High-quality sidewalks are an ideal tread for town walks. They have a smooth, level surface and are wide enough for two people to walk comfortably side by side and for two wheelchairs to pass. They should be buffered from automobile traffic by a 6- to 12-foot-wide landscaped tree median (figure 5.4). Wider walks and medians may be preferable when the walk follows a major collector street or arterial.

Figure 5.4. High-quality sidewalk with tree median. (Credit: Bill Neumann)

In shopping districts and other activity areas the walks should be a minimum of 8 feet wide, with a 3- to 4-foot clear zone for doorways.

Ideally there is also room for outdoor tables for dining and nooks with places to sit.

High-quality walks are associated with what are called complete streets, an approach to planning, designing, and building streets that enables safe access for all users, including pedestrians, bicyclists, motorists, and transit riders of all ages and abilities.[12]

Walkable Streets, Ped Lanes, Open Streets, and Quiet Streets

These are walkable segments created by the adaptation of low-traffic, low-speed streets. In the countryside this might be a back lane or an unpaved road (figure 5.5). In town it could be a local street that is safe and comfortable for walking (figure 5.6). In some instances, a 5-foot-wide painted pedestrian lane defines the walking space.[13] Traffic calming treatments such as chockers and chicanes, which basically narrow or undulate the traffic lane to slow traffic, make excellent walkable streets. Blocks designed as slow streets or woonerfs, where the road is primarily a pedestrian space with only very slow local traffic allowed to enter, serve this purpose too.[14]

Figure 5.5. Country road as a trail. (Credit: Bill Neumann)

Road diets may facilitate slow streets by modifying a street that is much wider than it needs to be (see figures 5.7 and 5.8). Wider-than-necessary streets are common, particularly in suburban areas. Not

Figure 5.6. In-town walkable street. (Credit: Robert Searns)

Figure 5.7. Fat street before road diet. (Credit: Bill Neumann)

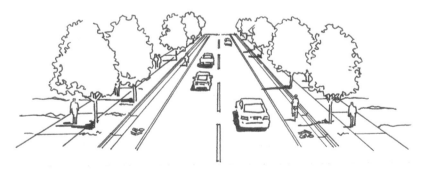

Figure 5.8. Fat street after road diet. (Credit: Bill Neumann)

only are way-too-wide roads pedestrian unfriendly, they add significant costs when it comes to repaving or snow plowing. Regardless of the policies and politics, it never hurts to propose an alternative. To do this, it will help to have a traffic engineer on your team. Road diets can improve walkability and, in some instances, offer space along street edges to create roadside linear parks (see *Linear Roadside Parkway Strips* below).[15,16]

Alleys also make great walkable streets. Some may be narrow and congested, but they can offer interest and cultural benefits with places to eat, stay, or shop.[17,18] In each instance there must be good visibility and a suitable walking surface. In urban areas, lighting should be part of the infrastructure. Share-the-road signs, typically a yellow diamond with a pedestrian figure, alert both motorists and pedestrians to the joint use scenario.[19]

Greenways, Trails, and Linear Parks

A portion of a proposed grand loop or town walk can be a greenway or other type of linear park. This opportunity is more likely through urban or suburban areas. In the case of greenways, the pathway should be screened by vegetation and terrain to create a semi-wild feel—a buffer zone as depicted in figure 5.1—to enhance wildlife spaces and minimize ambient urban noise such as traffic.

Linear parks may be existing city facilities or may be found in planned subdivisions, many of which have extensive networks of green corridors. The ideal ones connect to larger regional trail networks. These may be 60 feet wide or more with interconnected pathways. Homeowner associations typically manage them in planned subdivisions. Some may be open to the public. Others may be restricted to residents and not usable. Whereas some communities require dedication of publicly accessible routes in the development approval process, others don't. It would be

ideal if all new development projects were required to provide intercon-
nectivity with adjoining regional trail routes.

Linear Roadside Parkway Strips

Some communities have incorporated landscaped linear parks along the
edges of main roads (figure 5.9). They may define entries to the development and serve as green spines. These spaces have well-landscaped grassy
areas, plenty of trees, possibly flower gardens, nooks with benches, and
possibly shelters where people can rest along the way. They might run
along one side of the street or both and range from 20 or 30 feet wide
to a couple hundred feet or more. In other instances, developers and
planning officials can incorporate this cross-section into future projects.
From a walking standpoint they are preferred to traditional landscaped
center medians. At least on busier streets, center medians are harder for
pedestrians to get to and noisier, with traffic passing on both sides.

Figure 5.9. Linear roadside parkway walk. (Credit: Bill Neumann)

Note that this section does not outline technical specifications,
which vary with the specific conditions and locations. Fortunately,
many resources are readily available with more detailed guidance.
These include manuals and guides and many excellent trails and streetscape plans prepared by various jurisdictions. Many can be found
online. For planning nearly every type of trail, *Trail Planning, Design,
and Development Guidelines*, published by the Minnesota Department
of Natural Resources, is one of the best guides. It is full of intricate

details, numerous cross-sections, and specifications.[20] For sidewalk and streetscape guidance, a great starting point is the US Federal Highway Administration publication *Course on Bicycle and Pedestrian Transportation*. *The Urban Street Design Guide* by the National Association of City Transportation Officials is another helpful publication.[21] See also the *Helpful Resources* list at the end of this book. Of course, when you're ready to prepare detailed plans and designs, always consult a design professional to determine the current best practice standards and to comply with regulations, which can vary from jurisdiction to jurisdiction.

Overcoming Barriers

Barriers are impediments that obstruct, impede, or discourage passage. Because, unlike greenways, grand loops and town walks don't follow established, grade-separated routes like rivers or rail routes, there are challenges with building loops, such as crossing roads or uneven terrain. Fortunately, many of these barriers can be worked around with the right combinations of improvisation and creative design. In laying out a route, the place to start is to identify barriers on your planning map and then sketch out solutions for each situation. This section describes some ways to approach a few of the most common situations.

Hard and Soft Barriers

Hard barriers are physical blockades that are simply insurmountable without modification. They include freeways, rivers, railroads, constricted road underpasses and tunnels without walkways, impassable terrain, private and restricted properties, and other obstacles that block travel. In many areas street layouts, particularly cul-de-sacs and dead-end streets, are barriers. Traversing a hard barrier is simply not possible without structural modifications or right-of-way acquisition.

There is a second order of barriers. Soft barriers include difficult, unpleasant, or potentially unsafe impediments. These could be high-traffic areas with very narrow or nonexistent sidewalks, places where the route needs to cross multilane traffic, roads that lack pedestrian-friendly crossing devices, midblock crossings, lack of convenient crosswalks, and constricted underpasses, to name a few. Another disincentive includes long stretches exposed to hot sun, high winds, isolation, or other unpleasant elements such as neighborhoods that don't feel safe due to low foot traffic, crime, or poor lighting. Expanses of unplowed snow and ice in winter also fit into this category.

Working around Hard Barriers

The least costly approach to working around hard barriers might be to find suitable, pleasant alternative trail alignments. Where that's not workable, a pedestrian bridge, tunnel, or other structural solution may do the trick. Of course, these are costly, and usually grade changes are needed to climb up and over or tunnel under the obstruction. On the positive side, the investment in a structure such as a bridge spanning a freeway could be a high-visibility, even iconic feature. In addition, it may take only a single pedestrian span or underpass to link a much larger network together, making the cost justifiable. At the cul-de-sac level it might take subdivision regulations requiring pedestrian connectivity between neighborhoods.

Figures 5.10, 5.11, and 5.12 show some of the ways various hard barriers can be overcome. It is by no means a comprehensive list, and in the real world, each situation is unique. But the examples can be enabling and inspire creative, adaptive solutions.

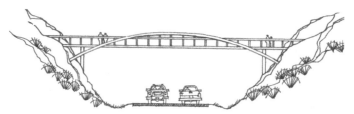

Figure 5.10. Grand loop pedestrian span on city edge. (Credit: Bill Neumann)

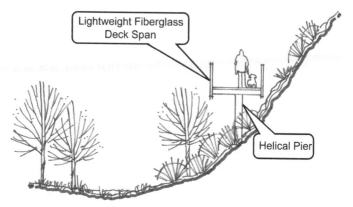

Figure 5.11. Traversing difficult terrain with lightweight fiberglass decking on helical piers. (Credit: Bill Neumann)

Figure 5.12. Passageway connecting cul-de-sacs. (Credit: Robert Searns)

Working around Soft Barriers

Most of the challenges with soft barriers involve at-grade road crossings where crossing busy streets is both daunting and potentially dangerous because of higher speeds, multilane roads, and complex traffic movements. Having high-quality walking routes and, even more importantly, establishing pedestrian-friendly networks overall with community-wide connectivity must include having safe, easy-to-use, pleasant crossings of streets throughout the system. Traffic engineers and planners aware of this problem should be called upon to develop workable treatments that can help people overcome the barriers created by busy streets.

The types of solutions vary depending on the specific conditions at any given crossing point, but there are commonalities as well. This starts with identifying and prioritizing logical places for people to cross and for traffic to stop, as well as locating crosswalks for visibility and functionality. Crossings should avoid multiple traffic movements, complex signals, and high-speed right turn lanes with intersections at right angles. In addition, depending on speeds and traffic volumes, there should be appropriate signage or signals at crossings. These include proper pavement markings in accordance with national and local design standards, such as advance stop bars or "shark's teeth" painted on the pavement to clearly advise motorists of the crossing.

On multilane and other busy roads, medians—pedestrian islands in the middle of the road—may be necessary, with appropriate signal timing (figure 5.13). There should be adequate time for people of all abilities to comfortably and safely make the crossing. In addition to signalization and markings, raised crosswalks and bollards at intersections have become popular in many places. Visibility is always important. Solutions such as curb extensions that make the pedestrian more visible to vehicles in the traffic lane can improve functionality of crossings. There should be adequate illumination at night.

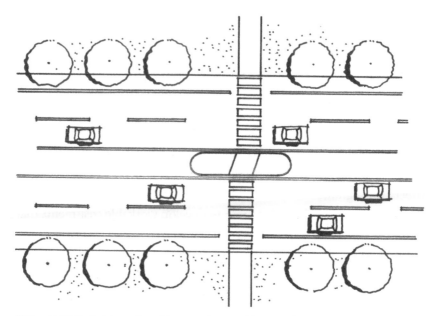

Figure 5.13. Pedestrian refuge islands reduce accidents and are a more comfortable way to cross. (Credit: Bill Neumann)

Of course, this is not a complete list of solutions; rather, they are examples of ways to approach pedestrian crossings. In all instances a professional engineer should be consulted. In the United States many of these can be found in, and should conform to, published standards in the *Manual on Uniform Traffic Control Devices (MUTCD)*.[22] Although many cities have implemented these changes, much more is needed. Where officials have not proactively engaged in addressing barriers, activist community organizations have improvised their own solutions. In Los Angeles, for example, where police statistics showed a pedestrian death every three days, a group started painting their own crosswalks. Groups in other communities have taken similar steps. Although this book does not advocate breaking laws, "guerilla engineering" is taking place. The book *Tactical Urbanism*, by Mike Lydon and Anthony Garcia,[23] cites examples. In Hamilton, Ontario, a citizen group initiated a "guerilla" traffic calming program, shaping a troublesome intersection this way. In another instance, a group called the Crosswalks Collective LA, noting the rapidly growing numbers of pedestrian injuries and deaths in Los Angles and frustrated by what they thought was the city's lack of response, began painting their own crosswalks. Although this approach could lead to being arrested, it has sometimes motivated officials to address the problems or at least look the other way.

Other solutions include pedestrian-operated stoplights called high-intensity activated crosswalk (HAWK) signal devices for higher-speed, higher-traffic, multilane and midblock crossings. They are less costly than a traditional traffic light. In other places where engineers deem it safe, a well-marked zebra crossing (like the one on the *Abbey Road* cover) works.

THE ART BECOMES THE CROSSING: ENGAGING ARTFUL INTERVENTION

With the guidance of the Bloomberg Associates Asphalt Art Initiative, led by urban designer David Andertons, the city engaged designers Quinton Batts and Vilde Ulset to define and reimagine three troublesome intersections with vibrant color schemes.

With the help of volunteers, they painted artful, attention-grabbing walking surfaces on the streets. In so doing they defined key walkability connections. The artful crossings were so visually impactful that follow-up studies found that the number of cars yielding to pedestrians increased by more than 40 percent. Even more impressive, analysis of twenty-two other asphalt art projects across the United States shows a 50 percent decrease in the rate of crashes involving pedestrians and cyclists and nearly a 30 percent increase in drivers yielding to pedestrians. Based on initial feedback from the Asphalt Art Initiative, it appears that this approach offers another low-cost tool for establishing town walk routes defined by applied art and make crossings safer simply by making them entertaining.[24]

Activating a Low-Use Area

Where the walks are in poor condition or nonexistent, it may be possible to adapt the street surface itself to become a walk. Going beyond this, prioritize the remedying of problem spots with landscaping and lighting. Policies that promote more diverse development and improvements that bring more street activity will help. Having more people present is a step toward a better ambiance. Projects such as the Indianapolis Cultural Trail and Denver's 5280 Trail took this approach, using the improvements to draw more people and businesses. Of course, a town walk project in and of itself is transformative, in effect, revitalizing its own corridor.

When that's not feasible, at least in the near term, there are less costly ways to make areas more appealing. Even the act of installing attractive wayfinding signage may help people get though a less desirable area. Other techniques embrace the very elements that may make an area seem less desirable. In laying out a pathway through an expansive, noisy, and hard-on-the eyes auto recycling area—some might call them junk yards—landscape architect Bill Neumann met with the operators and asked, "How can we tell your story?" The owners enthusiastically jumped on board, and the solution was to create rest areas with artistic displays built out of the very components found among the rusting automobiles piled up on the other side of the fence. Bill welded pickup truck tailgates, exhaust pipes, wheel rims, and other discarded parts into comfortable benches and sculptures for an entertaining display.

In the next chapter we will look at ways to effectively implement grand loops and town walks into real-world settings by creating effective, inspiring plans.

CHAPTER 6

Making a Plan

"You never really feel like you're building trails out here. . . .
Only finding them."

—Lawin Mohammad[1]

I was part of a group working on the Southern Nevada Regional Open Space Plan, which had a goal of creating a multidecade vision and framework for shaping the outdoors character of the rapidly developing Las Vegas Valley. A key focus was creating high-quality trail networks and preserving the character of the highly visible and "readily accessible" surrounding mountain and desert landscapes. After several days of extensive fieldwork familiarizing ourselves with the features of the greater Las Vegas area, we were sitting in the project office musing about what we saw.

Stepping up to the pad of paper with the plans, someone said, "We need to lively this plan up—a big idea!" and drew light bulb with a "smiley face." I sat there looking at the circular outline of the "face" on the pad and pictured the Las Vegas strip in the center and began to picture the surrounding mountains, desert, Lake Mead, Red Rock Canyon National Conservation Area, and other close-in iconic features that surround the city. Still looking at the circle, I recalled a plan that landscape architect Bill Neumann and I had done for Silverthorne, Colorado, a couple years prior, where we proposed a trekking trail encircling that mountain resort community. Dubbed the Silverthorne Loop, that hiking path would wind around the edges of town through the surrounding hills, linking national forest and wilderness areas. Suddenly, the "smiley face" took on a new character.

Two members of the group picked up sharpies and began sketching the open space and park features that ring Las Vegas and drew a line connecting them. With their marker lines, they showed the image of a trail running around the edges of Las Vegas, where city met the wildlands. "What do we call this?," someone blurted out. "We can't call it a 'greenway.' It runs through the desert! That landscape is red and brown!" "Let's call it the Vias Verdes Las Vegas," I quipped. A month later, Chuck Flink, the main author of the plan, boldly wrote a recommmendation calling for "the Vias Verdes Las Vegas," described as "an attractive transitional belt between the desert backdrop and the urbanizing area encircling the entire valley defined by an interconnected trail system."[2]

When we put the idea in the plan, which was adopted in 2006, it was just one of the recommended items. I don't think any of us expected the response we got to our bold idea. But then, a group called Outside Las Vegas enthusiastically embraced the Vias Verdes concept and set about to "develop a 113-mile . . . trail loop . . . around the Valley and link it to the to the existing trail network—connecting Southern Nevada from neon to nature." More appropriately named the Vegas Valley Rim Trail, the project was unanimously approved by the Las Vegas City Council in 2012 and by 2021 was more than 75 percent completed. Clearly ideas can come from both expected and unexpected places. The message is, find a way to plant the seed, nurture it with inspiration and credibility, and get the attention of groups with community ties, like Outside Las Vegas in this case.

From an Idea to a Built Reality

The first kernel of a future grand loop trail or a town walk could arise in multiple ways. Maybe you find it by just going out for a walk and getting inspired, like our forays into the landscapes surrounding Las Vegas. Or the idea could first show up in a community's trails or pedestrian master plan. In many cases the advocates have seen a similar successful project elsewhere. That's what happened with Denver's 5280 Trail, inspired by locals learning about the Heritage Trail in Indianapolis and New York's High Line, a pedestrian park built on a former elevated rail line structure.[3]

Unlike traditional greenways, grand loop and town walks usually cut across the grain. This leaves more freedom to envision potential routes, but there are new challenges because there is not a clear path like a river or rail route to follow.

In many ways laying out a pathway is like building a road. Both are routes that weave through the terrain. Planning a grand loop around a city is in many ways analogous to designing an interstate beltway. Town walk projects have similarities to city streets. You need to plot a route, design the proper components for the users, and fit the corridor into the setting. Planners need to address the topography, overcome barriers, secure rights of way, weave the route through existing land uses, and address many other factors such as vegetation, soils, utilities, and other infrastructure. The alignments need to be logical and the end products useful. And, as with road construction, you want to build a safe conveyance. Although there are similarities, unlike most roads, pathway projects are more challenging because trail builders have fewer resources and less clout at their disposal. From a design standpoint there is another big difference. In the case of building a road it's about getting from here to there. With a pathway it's also about the experience. Travelers on a road are enclosed in a vehicle, a bubble of metal and glass. Perception is pretty much limited to the visual. On a pathway, the person is more directly in touch with everything they can see, hear, smell, and feel than a motorist.

Experience with many communities that have pursued leading-edge projects reveals that there are key steps in going from concept to on-the-ground reality:

1. Plant the seed with an inspiring idea.
2. Draft a compelling vision statement and concept plan.
3. Get support and a management entity on board.
4. Assemble an action plan with achievable goals.
5. Make a budget.
6. Mobilize an effective organization.
7. Reach out, recruit leadership and assemble "worker bees."
8. Build community support.
9. Get the plan approved and adopted.
10. Garner resources.
11. Start building and complete logical segments step by step.

Tactical Considerations

Before laying out the planning process, there are some up-front tactical questions to keep in mind as you develop your ideas. Not all of the points listed below need to be answered at the conceptual phase, but is helpful to have an initial sense of the challenges so problems can be avoided or resolved, or workarounds found.

MAKING A PLAN 127MAKING A PLAN

Assess Buildability (Feasibility)

First, ask yourself whether the route can be established through the terrain. Can the alignment work, and is the project affordable? Given the lay of the land, could someone realistically walk this route and enjoy the experience? Are there ways to overcome barriers? Much of this starts with common-sense assessments such as looking at maps and field visits. Seeing whether projects have been built elsewhere in similar settings can also help.

Garner Support

This will come into play after a vision statement has been formulated, but it is never too early to get a few co-conspirators on board, to consult with and, at least, get a sense of acquiescence from vital players. Initially these might include a few influential advocates, business leaders, and elected officials. Also, work to recruit key people open to the idea in pivotal agencies such as planning, parks, and streets departments. Shop the idea around, maybe with a more formal presentation, to recruit potential allies and supporters. If official agencies aren't buying in, maybe they can be persuaded as more community leaders and influential people come on board.

Engage a Management Entity

The organization of project implementation has multiple modes of engagement. There is the startup group that introduces that idea and gets things moving. This group might be a special task force appointed by a mayor or governing council or an ad hoc citizens' group. There is the implementing entity that gets things designed and built. This could be a government agency such as a parks or public works department. Or a private foundation might carry out these tasks. And there is the owning entity, typically a parks department, responsible for accepting rights of way, general oversight and governance, and the ongoing maintenance of the project. This is the authority that houses the project. In many instances, these entities can be one and the same, and there may be public–private partnerships involved.

Once the key people are on board, it is helpful to identify the responsible entity. To move from a vision to reality there needs to be an agency or entity on board that takes ownership of the project, that houses the day-to-day nuts and bolts of securing funds, accepting rights-of-way grants, managing design and construction, and overseeing operations and maintenance. This might be a local parks or open space agency or a city streets department. A nonprofit organization might lead the way. The process could involve creating a whole new entity that provides these functions.

The Wolf River Conservancy teaming with the City of Memphis to build the Wolf River Greenway and the Denver Partnership teaming with the City of Denver to build the 5280 Trail are good examples of public–private partnerships. Alternatively, it could be a single public agency such as the Maricopa County Parks Department taking on building the grand loop trail around Phoenix. There may not be a lock on this kind of leadership at the start, but it's helpful to have a strategy and maybe a few influential supporters on board as the planning process begins.

There should also be an oversight committee consisting of public officials and citizen advocates. This group could include public works, parks, community development, and other representatives from transportation departments, transit districts, and public health. Ideally, the oversight group convenes on a regular basis—especially at key project juncture points—to review plans, progress, and policies. If a partnership with a nonprofit is involved, there needs to be a clear working agreement between the nonprofit and the respective jurisdictional entities where the pathway will be built. This might best be handled with a city council or country commission resolution that describes the project, the working agreements, and long-term management and maintenance provisions.

Rights of Way (Secured, Promised, or Likely)

Ideally, going into the planning process, the key routes have been secured, although in many instances some key rights of way take much longer to secure. There might be some key lands in public ownership that can be used, along with other connection potentials such as walkable roads. Phoenix, Las Vegas, and Denver have a number of large regional open space parks and state and federal land holdings, with potential to link them together. In these instances, the right-of-way picture was easier. Major public parks and open spaces can initially be identified on Google Maps, Google Earth, or similar apps, on local government geographic information system (GIS) maps, and on assessors' maps along with other parcels and lots, both public and private. The assessor maps and associated files also display property ownership details.

When you pull out your map to look for places to locate a route, your first question probably is where you can carve out the route. How do you build a grand loop that runs for a hundred miles or so through a landscape filled with private properties and other obstacles? For town walks it might be easier because of existing public rights of way. In either instance, having rights of way is at the core of establishing a route. They are the framework, the skeleton on which the trails and walks will be built.

Compared with traditional greenways, it is probably more difficult to acquire rights of way for grand loops and town walks. They cut across the grain of the landscape rather than following less developable corridors such as rivers, streams, floodplains, or even former rail routes. That's the challenging side. On the other hand, because our routes can, in places, follow existing public infrastructure such as sidewalks and roads, there is more flexibility. Fortunately, there are methods and strategies to establish routes. With the right solutions and agreements, they've been negotiated in many places across private lands. Routes have been secured through very difficult areas such as along the edges of railroad tracks, through water treatment plants, next to oil refineries, and even through working gravel mines. I know this because I was involved in acquiring some of these kinds of rights of way.

When thinking about establishing rights of way for walking, we are really talking about two different manifestations. The first is what most people envision, securing a legal right of passage through a property, in most cases from a private owner. The second is securing approval for pedestrian improvements that involve modifying public infrastructure such as streets and sidewalks.

In the case of grand loops, because they run primarily through less developed rural landscapes on city edges, there could be several factors working in our favor. First, there may be existing dedicated open spaces, state parks, or other large public spaces that offer routes. Land is usually cheaper. There may be more opportunities to incorporate trail corridors into new subdivisions and planned development projects, especially if there are supporting regulations. There are probably more opportunities to use walkable, low-traffic backcountry roads. It may be possible to incorporate walking facilities into dedicated road rights of way when they are platted, upgraded, or widened.

For town walks there is a different kind of ownership, usually a public entity. Deals can be made with a streets department or city engineer to secure permissions to alter and improve sidewalks, street crossings, and other infrastructure that has traditionally been designed and designated for automobiles. In most urban areas, street layouts and publicly owned street cross-sections have long been established. Many are confined within set limits, so there is not always room to widen a sidewalk or add a tree median. There are also engineering standards to address when installing pedestrian-friendly street crossings. In some instances, right-of-way needs will involve encroaching on abutting residential or business properties. Because of this context, be prepared with strategies to persuade city street engineers and elected officials to allow the changes. Also be ready to address concerns that the improvement will be too costly, impractical, or politically unpopular or perceived as too radical.

The Process

Having completed a vision plan, you should now have a map showing where the routes will probably go and the anticipated rights-of-way needs. This includes cross-sections of the corridor showing both the trail or walk and the surrounding acquisition areas needed for conservation and buffer swaths. Even if the plan is conceptual, there should be enough of an idea of the overall objectives and route alignment to initiate a practical acquisition strategy. The mapping should anticipate a back-and-forth process allowing for alternative routes and solutions should any of initial preferred alignments not be attainable. With the route mapping and cross-sections in hand, it's time to proceed with the next steps. These include the following:

- Assembling ownership documentation and parcel mapping
- Formulating an acquisition strategy
- Preparing consistent, nonthreatening messaging
- Negotiating
- Preparing the conveyance instruments
- Closing the deal

Ownership Documentation and Parcel Mapping

With a general idea of the routing in mind, the next step identifies the parcels involved. This includes both delineating private ownership and marking out street and sidewalk right-of-way lines. Knowing the adjacent land use is also important. Besides parcel maps, a simple Excel spreadsheet should be prepared, listing in sequence along the route the parcel numbers, the owners (with contact information), the parcel type and size, notes about the parcel such as zoning, and suitability for building such as floodplain and wildfire considerations. There should also be columns for follow-up tracking and notes. These will document conversations with owners or managers and the status of acquisitions. Large, usable public properties such as parks, public open spaces, and conservation areas should be highlighted both on the maps and on the spreadsheet. Color-coded boxes on the spreadsheet can help highlight types of ownership. Formatting this is personal preference, but the key is to have a way to list, follow up, and permanently document the process.

Much of the information to complete this task can be found at the tax assessor's office (most have a website). These files typically show the lot lines, the owner information, contacts, and other data. Many times, this information can be overlaid on an aerial map to get an idea of land uses, buildings, roads, floodplains, terrain, and zoning information.

Potential Funding Sources

Up-front funding is not a must at startup, but it is certainly helpful. It might be a small seed grant from a nonprofit or a staff and professional services commitment from an agency. Of course, at some point there needs to be a more significant stream of resources.

There are many forms of support beyond cash, such as donating rights of way, regulatory measures, and in-kind services. The following are ways to seek funding and other resources.

LOCAL GOVERNMENT APPROPRIATIONS AND SEED MONIES

These are directly budgeted funds, such as seed money, a challenge grant requiring that matching funds be raised, or an ongoing line item in a capital improvement budget. Nearly always a local public entity commitment is key. Granting agencies and donors want to see that local leadership is fully on board.

SPECIALLY DESIGNATED PUBLIC FUNDS

A sales tax increment can be dedicated to pedestrian and bicycle improvements, trails, and parks. This approach has been phenomenally successful in many places where a very small increment on sales can generate substantial funds that can be invested in infrastructure vital to the long-term health and economic wellbeing of the community.

In many cases such as sales tax; a bond issue; a dining, beverage, and lodging tax; or a special property tax assessment, voter approval is required. Clearly this approach requires a well-organized and funded campaign. It is essential to have a clear, inspiring, specific plan. Voters want to know how the money will be spent. Another effective tactic in this area is to incorporate the trails or walks project into a broader campaign, such as funding transportation, schools, or other programs that appeal to a wider voter base.

Charleston County, South Carolina, provides a great example of a program that envisions and enables creating a robust interconnected trail network. In his book *The Greenway Imperative*, Chuck Flink lays out, step by step, how leaders were able to get a sales and use tax program launched to implement an ambitious multidecade greenbelt and trail program. This included a 200-mile hiking and biking trail network interconnecting communities with open spaces; city, county, and state parks; and other outdoor places, including the region's treasured iconic wetlands. The tax referendums, starting in the early 2000s, also included broader benefits such as road construction and transit improvements. This partnering approach has been used in many such initiatives and is a lesson in making deals to win support from multiple constituencies.

Initially, the proposals failed to pass, but on the third attempt the measure was approved with a potential twenty-five-year stream totaling over $220 million. Chuck points out that a part of the reason for success in Charleston County was emphasis on the sense of place that people value as part of their identities. The Trust for Public Lands reports that, in many places, people vote for spending that supports green hometown projects—more than $56 billion in initiatives.[4,5]

An excellent example of this is the language in adopted development manuals for Central Park, a major mixed-use development built on the abandoned site of Denver's former Stapleton Airport. The key defining text reads, "Sidewalks will be provided adjacent to all streets. Special pedestrian amenities will be provided . . . to help mitigate pedestrian impacts of wider streets and intersections. . . . The development plan includes a number of parkways with significant landscaping that will encourage pedestrian use."[6] The specifications go on to state that sidewalks will be of "sufficient width to accommodate street trees [that] should be maintained along the majority of street frontage. Wider tree lawns are encouraged where possible as long as sidewalk continuity is maintained." The documents also specifically refer to walks that are detached and separated from the curb by tree lawns and street trees "to facilitate pedestrian and transit user movement through an interconnected network of detached sidewalks and convenient crosswalks."[7]

STATE CONSERVATION, RECREATION, AND URBAN DEVELOPMENT PROGRAMS

A number of states and provinces have funds that may be applicable to these kinds of projects. In Colorado, for example, the state lottery–funded Great Outdoors Colorado programs generate millions in acquisition and construction grants for trails and open space. California has a Recreational Trails Program, New York has a Park & Trail Partnership grant program, and British Columbia has a Community Culture and Recreation Program. These are just a few examples. Check to see what your state, province, or national government has. If there is not a program, it might be time to round up advocates and legislate one.

FEDERAL FUNDING

In the United States there have been transportation enhancement monies that include trails and sidewalks, typically administered by state transportation agencies. There is also the Land and Water Conservation Fund and various urban development programs. There have been stimulus grants and funding for health and fitness programs that help enable building trails and walks. It may be helpful to monitor federal websites to identify programs. *American Trails* typically posts alerts about various programs. Possible time delays or more stringent grant terms and requirements and associated administrative costs should be weighed in considering certain federal programs.

INDIVIDUAL, PHILANTHROPIC, AND CORPORATE GIVING

This type of funding includes gifts, grants, bequests, sponsored fundraising events, and other forms of giving. It may be helpful to identify or create a nonprofit "friends group" to seek and accept funds from private donors. In this realm, partnering with local employers, retailers, and other businesses may be helpful in funding projects, especially those that might benefit employees or customers engaging in active travel to get to or from work or shopping. In Memphis, the Hyde Foundation, working with the Wolf River Conservancy, provided major seed money for the Wolf River Greenway. In northwest Arkansas, the Walton Family Foundation provided the major funding for the 40-mile-plus Razorback

Greenway, and in New York State and southeast Michigan major private sector donors have facilitated projects of similar scale. Note that typically, corporate entities want to see a financial return on their funding, such as goodwill advertising, whereas philanthropic giving is often motivated by tax law requirements.

PARTNERING WITH OTHER ENTITIES WITH MUTUAL INTEREST

Finding people with mutual interest can be of significant benefit. Maybe it's a streets department, where sidewalk improvements or better pedestrian crossings could piggyback on a road project. It could be a utility, a firefighting entity, or an irrigation company wanting a trail to also serve as an access route. Try to envision what other uses your trail or walk could serve.

IMPROVISING, SCROUNGING, AND LEVERAGING

At the other end of the spectrum, people build projects by leveraging, scrounging, partnering, and piggybacking on other programs. The Turquoise Trail and the Transcarioca Trail, built largely by volunteers, stand out as examples.

Backup Plans

It's always good to have a plan B. This might mean laying out workable alternative routes now, even if they are less than perfect. With a longer-term phasing strategy, there could be a plan for completing revised routing or other improvements that would enhance the trail or walk in the future.

Preparing to Meet Challenges

Although you need to be realistic in anticipating obstacles, it's also important to also have an open, flexible mind. Be creative and persistent.

Many times, roadblocks that look impossible can be overcome. When a small group of us were first developing the Denver Platte River Greenway, no one had ever heard of a greenway. I heard people call the Platte River a "dump" where "no one would ever want to go." And in planning meetings with the Public Works and Parks departments I often heard some officials call the concept of a trail along the river "dangerous" and "a waste of money with so many other priorities." There was delay after delay in getting projects out to bid. Yet we persisted gently but firmly, setting a goal to get three pilot projects built. It took a couple of years, but once the ribbons were cut on the first improvements along the river, people could see the potential, and the greenway slowly took shape. Interestingly, there were gaps between the pilot project segments, but this probably worked to our advantage. The separated segments created a connect-the-dots mentality, making it easier to build the next phases, ultimately leading to a city-limit-to-city-limit continuous greenway. Today, the Platte River Greenway is one of the signature features of the region enjoyed by tens of thousands of locals and tourists. Our greenway consultant team has seen a similar phenomenon on the Memphis Wolf River Greenway and other projects. Get the vision out there, make deals, get proof-of-concept projects on the ground, and reach a critical mass where the endeavor takes on a life of its own.

The Planning Process

There are three key elements of many planning processes: visioning, preparing a concept plan, and writing a master plan. Trail projects are no exception. Sometimes the plan is specific to a particular project. In other instances, proposed grand loop or town walk projects could be a part of a larger citywide or countywide trail, park, or open space plan.

The level of planning can vary depending on the project. Some communities prepare complete and detailed master plans while others have built projects with just a vision, maybe a sketch or two. In every case, however, when it comes to construction, there should be drawings and specifications in sufficient detail to properly build what has been envisioned. Regardless of the approach, it is important that advocates strive for quality, and this means having a sufficient level of knowledge to guide the process, whether formally laid out in a detailed plan or based on the collective knowledge of those implementing the work.

Visioning

It is important to have a clear picture in mind of the experience you want to create. Initially, consider the setting, the opportunities, and the potential users. If it's a grand loop concept, have an idea of the scale and the terrain it will run through. If it's a town walk, determine whether it will it be a destination feature or a neighborhood amenity. As you formulate the vision, anticipate how it might resonate with the community and agency decision makers. Depending on the receptivity of key contacts, put some feelers into the community to test the idea. Later there will be a more extensive agency and public engagement process.

SKETCH IT UP

Next, it's time to put together a framework. This is the sketch phase. Because grand loops and town walks are overlays and don't have to follow established corridors, the entire urbanscape is your canvas. Maybe your idea is something you thought up while on a hike or walk around town. Maybe you saw an inspiring project somewhere. Maybe you'd like to see the concept incorporated into the overall trail masterplan for your area. Although you have an inkling of what it might be, I recommend starting at the intuitive level, unfettered by too much structure. You don't need artistic or drafting skills to do this, just a location, an idea, and some observations. Later, you'll get into the details. This is how projects such as the Maricopa Trail, the Vegas Valley Rim Trail, the Jeju Olle, and Denver's 5280 Trail got their starts. Someone had an idea or saw a similar inspiring project somewhere and sketched up a concept.

I suggest setting out to explore a potential route with a notepad, a street map, and a camera. Everything should fit in a daypack, because the idea is to go out there as freely and unburdened as possible. If you want, you can track your route with a walking app and take pictures on your phone. I think you'll be amazed at the ideas that will come to you just walking and sketching! You'll get the feel of a place, learn things from observing people, and quickly get a sense of the barriers and challenges you need to overcome. This initial step is not only fun but also the beginning of an iterative process starting with an inspiration and then moving on to a more substantial framework.

Write a Vision Statement

With the guidelines in place and some initial sketches, the next step is to formulate a vision statement and a concept plan that articulates your idea. It should take a form that can easily be conveyed to others, including key decision makers and officials as well as the general citizenry. Start by picturing what the pathway will look like when it's built, where it will go, who it will serve, and how it will change things for the better. The image will evolve during the process, but this initial articulation can convey and document a sense of what you want to accomplish. With the vision statement you want something that will plant the seed with advocates and decision makers. You want key people to embrace the idea, ultimately to secure a willingness to investigate the idea and get some startup funding and initial commitment of staff to move the idea forward.

A vision statement can be a half-page description, the "thirty-second elevator statement." Maybe there's a sketch or two. It should convey a compelling image of what can be accomplished, the benefits it will offer, particularly to local residents, and an encapsulation of what, hopefully, will become a shared community aspiration. Test it on a few confidants and tweak it as needed. Then shop it around to a broader circle of influential people such as civic leaders and agencies to get reactions so you can refine it and build support. Early on, work on making the case that the project will serve a broad cross-section of the populace, with equitable access and net benefits to all regardless of financial status. If there's an opportunity, the vision statement may be worked into other large-scale community planning efforts, such as a general trail or walkability master plan. Following are examples of vision statements. Actual statements will vary, of course. Consider local needs, aspirations, and challenges in writing what will best resonate and gain support in your venue.

A grand loop trail vision statement might read like this:

> Establish a grand loop hiking trail that encircles the metro area along its edges where city meets countryside. It will be a close-in, soft-surface trail with a backcountry feel enjoyed at a walking pace. It will be a fully integrated, continuous trail offering a spectacular experience, readily accessible to a diverse cross-section of the community. It will support lightweight, "day pack" travel with conveniently spaced places to find provisions and overnight accommodations for those making a multiday trek. This grand loop trail can, in effect, become a new overlay regional park. As appropriate, and where there would be minimal conflicts, other trail uses such as bikes and horses may be accommodated.

For a town walk it might say,

> Create a 3-mile-long [or other length you are planning for], readily accessible, high-quality walking route that encircles the [downtown, the historic district, or other focal point] with safe, pleasant, shaded sidewalks and street crossings. There will be conveniently

placed rest spots and easy access to shops and restaurants. There will be artistically designed mile markers to guide the way. The project will increase walkability and serve as a proof of concept for other pedestrian-friendly projects that serve [name the city]. In effect it will also become an overlaid park serving both city residents and out-of-town visitors.

When addressing doorstep walks, the statement is a bit different in that it advocates for a citywide system in pursuit of walkability. It could read like this:

To promote better health, fitness, cleaner air, and community revitalization, implement a series of walkability policies and pilot projects—programs that will offer people opportunities for more barrier-free, safe, and pleasant walking [and biking if applicable] from their doorsteps. This includes a "complete streets" program with high-quality sidewalks, safe street crossings, tree medians, and resting spots with benches and other amenities. The system will also encourage and enable more walkable travel to workplaces, transit, schools, shops, parks, and civic spaces, around neighborhoods and to other destinations.

Although there are countess examples and ways a visioning process can work, an interesting one is the creation of the Razorback Greenway in northwest Arkansas. In 2010 a few of us greenway planners were asked by staff of the Walton Family Foundation, who wanted to improve the quality of life in that area, to engage in a brainstorming session. We assembled a group and called ourselves the Green Team, joined with local civic and agency leaders, and during a two-day workshop conjured up the idea of a 35-plus-mile trail running along the spine of the region from Bentonville to Fayetteville, connecting five cities together.

Shortly afterward we assembled a team of community and agency representatives, laid out maps and newsprint pads, and in a day-long session assembled the vision. We estimated a cost of $38 million to secure the rights of way and build it. Although there was resistance in some quarters, the community by and large embraced the idea, and more formal planning and fundraising got under way. The Walton Family Foundation committed $3.75 million to help leverage a federal grant and later contributed additional money, and the local communities signed on. Nine months after the vision statement and concept map took shape, the project was fully funded. The ribbon opening the Razorback Greenway trail was cut in 2015. Although this vision-to-reality process had the exceptional benefit of Walton Foundation support, there are many other examples of this process working, whether by philanthropical impetus or a commitment of public funds. The key is to get the idea out there and present an inspiring, compelling case. And it doesn't hurt to recruit some influential support, although a project can also work with more modest partnership models.[8]

Preparing a Concept Plan

At this stage it is important to make the case clearly conveying why the project is needed and, importantly, that it can be done. With the initial vision statement and sketch plan in place, the next step is to prepare a concept plan. The concept plan is a brief description and overview of the vision, typically including the vision statement, an appealing easy-to-read map of the project route, photos and illustrations, a summary of the benefits, a list of next steps, and a call for action. The concept plan could be presented in a brochure or a small booklet. There should also be a compelling PowerPoint presentation or maybe a brief video presentation in the package. The content should be formatted for an online presence, a website set up, and social media pages secured. The

Downtown Denver Partnership's website that depicts the Denver 5280 Trail plan and the Wolf River Conservancy website that describes the Wolf River Greenway trail project area are excellent examples.[9,10]

Ideally, at this point, there is a core group of initiators who agree on the ideas and there is some seed money to put a package together that will convey the vision and win support. Although a concept plan is not yet a detailed master plan, people with writing and graphic skills should be engaged at this point to help professionally prepare the materials.

The materials should emphasize existing opportunities such as open spaces that could be linked together. Where there are potential adjacent property ownership questions, the route mapping should be broad, not site-specific. If circumstances enable it, stress that the effort is about closing gaps such as how existing greenways, trails, sidewalks, and walkable on-street segments could be strung together into a bigger network. With the concept plan in place, you're ready to take it on the road to build support and recruit participants.

Preparing a Master Plan

In many cases a project can proceed with just a concept plan. For the Maricopa County Regional Trails System, however, a detailed master plan had to be prepared that fully described a grand loop trail around Phoenix. This process is pretty much the same format as for any trail, greenway, or pedestrian facility plan. Although the work products will probably be published in printed form, there should be easily accessible online versions available. Master plans may have different forms, lengths, and formats, but there are common essential elements.

THE MISSION STATEMENT

This states specifically what the plan sets out to accomplish. It is the vision. If you prepared a conceptual plan, then you have already written the mission statement. See the examples of vision statements earlier in this chapter.

BACKGROUND AND PURPOSE OF THE PLAN

This overviews the reason for the plan, the intended users, who authorized the plan, what the plan sets out to accomplish (the goals), and other contextual information. This element should also include the programming of the plan, the list of the proposed improvements: the pathway itself, rest areas, furnishings, wayfinding, interpretive and artistic elements, street crossings, decks and bridges, landscaping, and other elements.

GUIDING PRINCIPLES

These set out the standards of quality for the proposed improvements and the guardrails for compatibility of the planned improvements with their settings. Chapter 4 sets out the guiding principles for grand loops and town walks.

SITE ANALYSIS INFORMATION, INCLUDING OPPORTUNITIES AND CHALLENGES

This step begins with gathering maps and data about the planning area. There will be layers of maps, starting with base mapping that is then overlaid with an analysis of the existing conditions, such as topography, environment, flora and fauna, land uses, existing trails, existing or planned infrastructure, and other factors that affect the route. The scale of the base mapping will vary depending on the situation. For a grand loop, 1 inch to a mile or more may work. For a town walk it might be 1 inch to 100 feet or less. The key is that there is enough detail to covey the general site conditions. For construction drawings the scale will be much more detailed. Two recognized designers, Bill Neumann, with DHM Design Landscape Architects, and Tony Boone, with Tony Boone Trails, offer advice on assembling materials for site analysis.

Bill, who has designed many greenways, trails, and streetscape projects, suggests starting with online Google Earth maps. He notes that they're free and a quick way to set up a base file for your project. They provide aerial imagery with road labels and information about local features. Online US Geological Survey maps are also available. They show topography, roads, streams, boundaries, and other physical features. He adds that in many places, city, and county GIS databases also are great way to obtain quick mapping online, including land ownership parcels, municipal boundaries, and other easements. Bill's firm uses drones to get higher-resolution maps in some instances.

Tony, whose focus is on building natural surface trails, also suggests the sources Bill uses. He adds that he has found drone data to be increasingly useful. He suggests engaging a drone service. Some of the drone technology is so detailed, he says, "that you can see the fish in the streams." He likes having 1-foot contour maps, but for planning, he says you can work with large-scale gradient lines of 5 to 10 feet. An online search will reveal several firms that provide comprehensive drone data services.[11]

Ownership Mapping and Documentation

This includes mapping out the land ownerships, showing the boundaries of each significant parcel. The names of the specific owners can be documented by parcel on a spreadsheet listing the addresses, contact information, and follow-up notes. This information should not be publicly released except for, perhaps, a map that shows only publicly owned land and large parcel boundaries without the owner names disclosed.

Field Reconnaissance

An essential task is going out and "kicking the dirt" and includes a field inventory of existing and potential route alignments. The goal is to tour as much of the route as possible on foot. When there are time constraints or where certain segments are inaccessible due to private ownership or other impediments, field investigation by car is an option. This could include driving along or close to possible trail routes and stopping at key spots to get a sense of the ambiance. As Tony Boone suggests, drones may be useful in this step, being cautious not to alarm or offend property owners. Global Positioning System (GPS) tracking can be helpful, and there should also be a thorough photo inventory with each photo linked to GPS location, listing the coordinates, the date taken, and other relevant information.

PUBLIC PROCESS

There is the general populace, affected property owners, agency people, and stakeholders including user groups and associations. Every effort should be made to identify key groups such as directly affected property owners and reach out to them individually. Ideally public forums or open houses are held at three stages: after the initial site analysis is completed, when draft concepts are prepared, and when the final draft plan is ready. Anticipate possible public engagement when the plan goes to the governing board entity for final approval and adoption. I recommend that the public sessions be informal, not held as "hearings." My colleagues and I usually conduct them as participation sessions where maps are laid out on tables, markers provided, and folks invited to share suggestions and marked-up drawings. Maps and other design images may also be posted on the walls, but under no circumstances should routes be specifically drawn through individual properties. There may be a PowerPoint presentation at the beginning of the session to orient people, but then the audience can go to the worktables to share their thoughts. All input is documented, and the records should be saved. The public process should be supported by a clearly and attractively designed online presence. An important part of the public process is to have broad, diverse outreach engaging different income and ethnic groups. Local planning officials may be helpful in providing contact information for reaching different stakeholder organizations. Chapter 7 has additional details on outreach.

CONSIDER CREATING AN ADVISORY COMMITTEE

Although this is not always done, assembling an advisory group can be very helpful in getting input and building support. These people can be recruited from the ranks of key interest groups, agency staff, business leaders, and other decision makers. This committee should be kept well apprised on the progress of the project. Their input should be openly received and responded to. In addition to the committee members, a list should be kept of other interested parties such as advocacy groups, elected officials, and other key agency staff, and they too should be routinely briefed. This group ideally will continue on into the implementation phase after the plan is published.

LAYOUT AND ALIGNMENT PLAN (SOMETIMES WITH ALTERNATIVE ALIGNMENTS)

This includes a drawing that plots out on a map where the pathway will go. There should also be a program prepared, listing the recommended improvements that go with the trail, such as rest areas, trailheads, and other features. It gives the public, agency staff, and other stakeholders a chance to see the ideas and comment. If necessary, there may be alternative routes shown. Again, avoid site-specific lines that go through private properties.

DESIGN GUIDELINES FOR COMPONENTS, FIXTURES, AND FURNISHINGS

This includes depictions of all key improvements from a cross-section of the pathway itself to rest areas and other structures. It also includes a wayfinding plan depicting the recommended signage, mile markers, and, if applicable, artistic elements. It may be in an appendix to the plan or integral in the report.

DRAFT MASTER PLAN REPORT

Once the draft alignment map and program elements have been reviewed, revised, and approved, it is time to prepare a draft report that documents the findings and recommendations. It could be printed or posted online as well as presented in a second round of public engagement meetings.

FINAL MASTER PLAN

After input on the draft plan is received, the final documents are prepared. They should be clear and concise, with attractively drawn maps and renderings of the components. The report should not be too lengthy, and there should a summary version, ideally in an attractive brochure format.

Cost Estimates

These are planning-level estimates of costs used for creating a project budget. They are not yet exact engineering estimates but should be accurate enough for requesting funding appropriations and grant writing.

The first question an elected official or other decision maker is likely to ask is, "How much will it cost, and how will it be paid for?" And yes, although you must be prepared to respond in a credible manner to the monetary questions, costs are only part of the equation. I prefer to call the financial aspects budgeting because, besides the costs, you want to identify the revenue sources that will pay for the project. You also want to address the return on investment to the community. For any proposed expenditure this is the more complete picture, and it provides perspective. Let's start with the costs.

First, realize in making a pitch that it's important to keep the costs in perspective. A $20 million price tag to build a grand loop trail may sound like a lot but maybe not so much compared to the cost of building a new sports arena, a city park, or a freeway interchange. The estimate to upgrade a single interchange in the San Jose, California, area is $1 billion.[12] Although no one wants to propose or try to justify extravagant spending, the question is not so much the price tag but how it fits into the overall capital budget of a city or county and whether there are revenue resources potentially available to offset the costs. Costs and revenues—that's a budget.

Because the character of a grand loop or town walk can vary depending on the level of improvements made, there is no rule for cost estimating. It requires checking comparable prices on similar projects, locally or in other communities, and ways to pay for them to come up with a ballpark tally of expenses. Doing this, early on, can go a long way toward building credibility and commanding the respect of elected officials and other decision makers. These start by breaking out the types and categories of expenses involved. Here are five key cost categories:

Project management and development. This includes the staff or consultant services needed to oversee the entire effort from concept plan to ribbon cutting. It also includes grant writing. Depending on the project scope and complexity, costs will range from the part-time services of one individual to possibly a team of people.

Planning and design. Consider the landscape architect and engineering fees along with special and technical services such as surveying, mapping, environmental assessments, construction supervision, permitting, legal fees, and quality control. This element might run from 8 to 15 percent or the construction costs.

Right-of-way acquisition and approvals. These are the costs of purchasing the rights of way and associated conservation lands. The acquisition might be an easement, a permit, or an outright purchase of the land needed. Added to this are costs for negotiation and preparation of the deeds and other legal instruments. Of course, this will vary significantly depending on the routing.

Construction costs. These will vary significantly depending on what is to be built. A natural surface trail is much cheaper than a paved hike/bike path or a total street makeover. There is no single formula, but once you have an initial plan in place and know the approximate mix of pathway surfaces and components needed, you can begin to calculate per-foot costs. Cost factoring for this stage might range from less than $10 to $3,000 or more per foot depending on the components. Typically, numbers are available from recent unit bids on similar local projects and can be found online. Sources such as American Trails can also be helpful because they post costs for construction from various sources. Be sure the prices you use are current.[13]

One shortcut method my colleagues and I have used in these initial stages is to lay out the route on a map, note terrain and other difficult areas, and mark out segments by degree of difficulty. The next step is to categorize the construction challenges, such as steep terrain, and break out the levels of complexity from "simple," meaning a basic natural surface trail on stable surface or sidewalk repairs needed here and there, to "intermediate," such as needing a paved path, to "difficult," meaning retaining walls and hand railings, to "complex," where a pedestrian span or suspended deck is needed. With different-colored markers, we mark off and measure the lengths of each type of complexity, total the lengths by category, and rough out a total cost. This preliminary pricing should suffice for initial budgeting and grant writing. Later in the process, the landscape architect or engineer can prepare the detailed costs based on final designs and recent construction bids.

Operations and maintenance. Here the plan overviews the operational costs, including routine maintenance tasks, patrols, long-term upkeep, and other anticipated expenses once the project is built. Rest assured, someone will ask about the upkeep costs, even if there is a big grant for construction. If not addressed, maintenance cost anxieties can be a deal killer. These expenses include not only the obvious considerations such as repairs and litter pickup, but police patrol, rescue, and liability coverage. For planning purposes you can rough-calculate annual upkeep costs per mile. There are multiple resources for estimating this, including information from similar projects, streets and parks departments, and reliable sources including American Trails and the Rails-to-Trails Conservancy. Depending on complexity, anticipate annual costs ranging from less than $2,000 for a more primitive trail to $20,000 or more per mile per year for a more developed facility. For town walks, because they are much shorter, although per-foot costs tend to be high, the overall annual operational budget should be significantly less than that of grand loops, except possibly in the case of extensively developed town walks such as the Denver 5280 Trail or the Indianapolis Heritage Trail.

A price tag, even in the tens of millions, can be a lot less painful and discouraging if there is a credible plan in place to cover building and maintaining the improvements. Even better, it is helpful to show a projected return on the taxpayers' investment. So be ready with both sides of the balance sheet when taking your project idea to the decision makers.

Have an itemized strategy in place with potential streams of money identified. Consider grant potentials; local, state, federal, and philanthropic monies; and realistic in-kind services including volunteers and improvements such as street and sidewalk paving by the respective departments. Investigate other types of financing such as bond issues, sales and lodging taxes, and special taxing districts and assessments. Factor in the potentials for right-of-way dedications by developers building new projects as part of the subdivision regulatory process. Try to list realistic projections of the potential sources.

Convey the premise that trails and walks projects are revenue generators. There is a return on investment. The benefits include increased real estate values, tourism revenues, and guide service, restaurant, outfitter, and lodging income. Also, consider the reduction in healthcare costs with a more fit population. Although filling out this part of the "balance sheet" is more abstract, there are many studies that detail the likely returns. It is useful to have a few of these to quote in your presentations. The Rails-to-Trails Conservancy reported in 2019 that research shows that "investment in trails, walking and biking infrastructure, delivers potential economic benefits of $138.5 billion annually."[14]

A University of Las Vegas economic study concluded that the Vegas Valley Rim Trail–related spending by local or nonlocal visitors "would result in total value-added income" of roughly $477,089,046 to the southern Nevada economy and generate 7,544 jobs in southern Nevada.[15]

Another study published by the Indiana University Public Policy Institute suggests that the Indianapolis Cultural Trail, certainly an inspiration for town walks, increased property values around it by 148 percent—more than a billion dollars—between 2008 and 2015 and that the average expenditure of each visitor was $53.[16] There is also the more intangible, yet very real, benefit of making your community a better place to live.

Implementation Recommendations Including an Action Plan

This section discusses potential funding sources and leadership scenarios for getting the project built. It should also include an action plan, a step-by-step guide that can stand on its own, laying out the specific steps, costs, priorities, and completion dates. The action plan includes a roster of projects. The roster is a list of logically doable projects with budgets and deadlines. Things should happen quickly. This element is important. Even the best, most inspiring plan risks oblivion if it is left to gather dust or is forgotten. Things need to get built! The scale depends on the resources and level of public support, but in all cases the timing needs to be expeditious. This part of the plan should also include policy and regulatory recommendations including incentives for developers and other decision makers to support implementing the plan. Start the list with the low-hanging fruit, the pieces that can more easily be put in place, such as linking two existing trail segments or installing a safe street crossing. The roster of projects gives the plan legs and demonstrates a commitment to making something happen in a logical, feasible, and timely way.

Gearing Up to Move from a Plan to a Project

Once the plan is finalized, it is time to make final presentations and seek approval and adoption. This will probably be with the official governing body or bodies, or it may be adoption by the leaders and board of the nongovernment implementing organization, or both if it's a public–private partnership. Official adoption is especially important to provide legal support for implementing regulatory and incentive measures such as subdivision provisions that facilitate dedication of rights of way and funding as appropriate. In addition, the appropriate jurisdictional elected officials and staff such as transportation and parks departments should sign off.

The master plan is then handed off to the landscape architects and engineers who will prepare the actual drawings and specifications, also known as bid documents. These are not produced in the planning process, but the plan should be clearly written out to facilitate the preparation of construction documents. Besides addressing the field conditions including the opportunities and challenges of the proposed trail corridor, it is helpful to have a clearly laid-out compendium of the recommended components and furnishings such the pathway surface, trailheads, and other built elements.

Once the planning efforts have formulated the vision and detailed the recommendations, the next step is to move from ideas on paper to on-the-ground improvements. At this stage, in addition to securing official adoption and startup funding, implementing the action plan and continuing public engagement are important. Feasible proof-of-concept projects can show what can be done. Timely completion of logical segments will establish enthusiasm and credibility, especially projects that demonstrate the value and benefits. Projects should not be perceived as "trails to nowhere" or otherwise perceived as marginally useable. They should be replicable and catalytic in that they inspire completing more segments to continue the effort. Ideally, usable pieces are built and opened every year. Nothing will establish the credibility of a plan like the timely cutting of ribbons on projects people can use.

Continuing to Engage the Community

In addition to public participation during the planning process, building broader, longer-term support is an important next step in moving from planning to implementation. Although not everyone in the community needs to be a participant or embrace the plan—there are always those who oppose nearly every kind of plan—there should be an essential, critical mass core of acceptance and enthusiasm. This means continuing engagement with influential leaders, trail advocates, property owners, and other stakeholders. It also means maintaining a media presence, including an up-to-date website and news releases at key junctures such as grant announcements, groundbreakings, and ribbon cuttings. Chapter 7 goes into more detail regarding implementation and public engagement strategies.

CHAPTER 7

Building Support, Engaging the Public, and Motivating Trail Users

*"Sadly, teaching, and convincing people is not enough.
We must build a more walkable world, so people want to
and are able to get out there every day!"*

—Mark Fenton, Host, PBS America's Walking Series

To become a reality, any plan needs a constituency, particularly among those who have access to resources and decision making regarding approvals. If there is a master plan involved, hopefully there has already been a successful public engagement process in crafting that plan. Once you have reached the implementation stage, you want to keep people informed with stories in the media, periodic updates to stakeholders, and other interested parties giving them the opportunity to comment. And always be tuned into and prepared to address any public or agency decision makers' anxieties or concerns. If a vote is needed for something such as approval of a bond issue, a proactive campaign will be needed.

Add to this constituency-building element the value of branding. Having a catchy moniker for the project that conveys what it is and captures its benefits can be a huge help. The Heritage Trail, the Turquoise Trail, and the Vegas Valley Rim Trail say something about those places. So too do the Jeju Olle and the Transcarioca Trail brands. In a word or two, there's a message about what the trail is that resonates with the locals—and visitors. In the Denver instance, "5280" tells you the path is 1 mile high and, indirectly, 5.2 miles long. "Olle," in Korean dialect, means "the small alley leading from your house to the street" instilling the notion that that 271-mile loop around Jeju Island is also your own intimate pathway, like the walk from your front door. And in Brazil a "carioca" is someone or something from Rio. *Transcarioca* conveys the defining essence of Rio de Janeiro. So give your project a brand.

Public Engagement

With the concept and action plan in hand, it's time to reach out to trail advocates and to key individuals in the business communities, including real estate, travel, and tourism groups. This stage includes both building support and getting reactions, critiques, and suggestions that can strengthen the plan and its relevance and reception. In addition to having the materials in hand, it is important to have well a few well-versed people with presentation skills lined up to reach out to community leaders and officials as well as making presentations to the public. The most effective presentations involve a live person speaking to the group. Assemble a media package including a news release and establish an online presence.

When thinking about making the case, ask yourself, "What are the problems this project will solve?" Not enough access to high-quality walking and hiking places? Overcrowded existing outdoor facilities? Traffic and fuel costs to reach more remote trails and outdoor places? Lack of diverse, equitable access? Epidemic obesity and other health problems? In presenting the plan, emphasize the solutions and the opportunities the plan offers.

Also anticipate potential community concerns and possible points of resistance and be prepared to address them. Some of these could be costs, taxes, impacts, and gentrification displacing people. Be prepared for local parochialism, particularly when proposing a large-scale regional project involving multiple jurisdictions. Some may perceive your idea as competing with other projects and priorities.

There will be regulations to comply with, and there will always be fears about safety, crime, property and privacy, and impacts on traffic. However, this should not put a damper on things. These obstacles are not uncommon, and they're not deal killers. They can be overcome, but it's important to go into the process thinking about these concerns and ways to address them.

The next step is assembling a circle of influential supporters and effective, credible leadership. There are three aspects to leadership: the instigator, the champion, and the worker bee. These might be embodied in one person, but it's probably a group of effective people.

The instigator is probably the person who first envisioned the idea and now is putting the implementation effort into action. This person (or group) conceived of the concept and is committed to seeing it through to completion. This might be a private citizen, an elected official, an agency staff person, or other key individual. Importantly, they must have communication skills and credibility.

The champion is a committed person (or a small group) who will pursue the vision. It could be a private citizen, maybe an elected official or a business leader who has both the skills and the clout to promote, incentivize, trade favors, and, where needed, cajole. Sometimes, like Suh Myung-sook (Suki), who created the 250-plus-mile grand loop trail around the circumference of Jeju Island, South Korea, the champion is the one who conceived of and initiated the endeavor. In other instances, it is an influential person who embraces the idea and then leads the implementation effort. In Denver, the champion was Joe Shoemaker, an influential Colorado politician (also the powerful chair of the State Joint Budget Committee and former city public works director) who made the Platte River Greenway happen. In each instance the champion should have respectability and, ideally, some clout.

In each instance these champions led the organizations to implement their projects. Suki created the Jeju Olle Foundation that spearheaded that effort, and Shoemaker served as the chair of a mayor-appointed committee tasked with implementing the Denver greenway. The Shoemaker Committee later became the Board of Directors of the Greenway Foundation, a nonprofit group that assumed leadership of the private side of that public–private greenway effort. There are numerous other examples of champions. If you're not fortunate enough to have this type of person in place, then look to the ranks of public-spirited citizens, businesspeople, or political leaders who have a passion for the plan and who would be committed to its realization over the long term.

In another instance, the "champion" was not one person but three influential and dedicated elected officials from three different jurisdictions working in concert. Jim Daily, the former mayor of Little Rock, describes how the now-88-mile-plus Arkansas River Trail was created. He said, while modestly crediting many, that he, Pat Hays, the mayor of North Little Rock, and Floyd "Buddy" Villines, the Polaski County judge, formed a team. They pursued a vision that resulted in building 16 miles of trail along the Arkansas River that involved converting railroad bridges and a dam into major pedestrian crossings, linking Little Rock and North Little Rock. They wrangled the bridge crossings from the railroads and dam operators, got capital funds appropriated by their respective boards, and engaged the respective parks departments in building the trail. Jim is still involved in expanding the system into a larger loop network.

With the leadership and a core organization in place, it's time to secure some seed money and engage a professional project manager: the worker bee. This individual, or group of individuals, executes the project day-to-day. This could be a parks department planner or the staffer of an advocacy or nonprofit organization. The position could be a salaried employee or a contracted development consultant retained to do the job. This person or group is tasked with finalizing the plans, implementing built projects on time and within budget, and ensuring continuation and enhancement of supportive policies, programs, and events that engage and inspire the public.

Expertise in planning, fundraising, budgeting, right-of-way acquisition, and overseeing design services will be needed. As things progress, other professional services including design, engineering, and legal expertise will be needed. Some of the skill sets and tasks of a project manager include

- Oversight and advocacy to complete project tasks
- Recruiting, assembling, and coordinating the range of professional services needed, from landscape architects to engineers to legal services
- Developing a more formal master plan if needed
- Promoting community advocacy by working with citizens, community leaders, businesspeople, property owners, and other stakeholders to communicate the vision and build support
- Securing and assembling agreements, legal charters, and other institutional elements such as a land trust of conservancy to direct the process
- Garnering resources and funds, including grant writing, early on and getting seed money to build a pilot project
- Building and maintaining effective partnerships between agencies and jurisdictions

• Ensuring policy consistency of ordinances and government programs such as street and road planning with implementation and stewardship objectives

The project manager must have capabilities on these multiple fronts, able to lead and coordinate a team of designers, fundraisers, right-of-way negotiators, and contractors to see the project through. There should be both technical and people skills. The project manager should be someone who will embrace the project and see it through to completion.

Types of Management Structures

There are several models of addressing trail oversight, ownership, and governance. Often, there is mix of ways to engage resources and public and private involvement. At one end of the spectrum, there are large, publicly funded and implemented programs. Then there are the more modest, incremental efforts involving both government and nongovernment entities, perhaps where a nonprofit trail advocacy group partners with an agency such as a park department. At the other end, we have improvised, scrappy efforts. In every type there have been notable successes and takeaway lessons.

Single-Agency Lead

In this model, a government agency leads and manages the project. In many instances, large-scale green infrastructure and trail programs are envisioned, funded, and implemented in this way by a single entity. It could be a citywide, countywide, or metro-wide program. The Maricopa Country Trail, which forms a 315-mile grand loop trail around the edges of metro Phoenix, is a good example The effort took off in earnest when the County Board of Supervisors saw the need and made a $5 million dollar commitment of county funds. Trail construction began in 2007.[1]

A single lead entity might arise from a voter initiative, as was the case in Jefferson County, Colorado, and many other places where voters approved an open space sales tax. In Jefferson County, this funding led to the creation of a separate department responsible for creating a network of open spaces and trails throughout the county.

Multiple Agencies and Jurisdictions in Partnership

In this model, several government agencies form a coalition or an intergovernmental agreement to lead and manage the project. The Northwest Arkansas Regional Planning Commission coordinated an effort for the 40-plus-mile Razorback Greenway running from Bentonville to Fayetteville. Completing the trail required several cities to join in and cooperate with the completion of segments through their jurisdictions. In this instance major funding came from the Walton Family Foundation and a federal transportation grant leveraged by the Walton funds.

Public–Private Leadership

In this model a public entity partners with a citizens' action group or nonprofit that helps promote the project and raise funds. In many instances, the private entity is more proactive in planning, promoting, and fundraising. In other cases, the government entity takes more of the lead. Both models can work depending on the players and the circumstances. A private-side lead has some advantages in this scenario, however. For example, a public entity such as a parks department may be busy with multiple demands, whereas a private partnering entity can be more focused on the specific project and often be more politically and financially free to promote the project and to seek and manage funds from private donors, particularly if a tax deduction benefit to donors is in play.

The Wolf River Greenway in Memphis fits this model. The Wolf River Conservancy, a nonprofit group with substantial financial support from the Hyde Foundation, partnered with the City of Memphis to build a legacy trail along the length of the Wolf River on the north side of the city. Connections with other trails in Memphis, including along the Mississippi on Mud Island, the Memphis/Shelby Farms Greenline trail, and other segments, suggest the potential of a Memphis grand loop or multiple loops one day.

The Indianapolis Cultural Trail is another example. Between 2007 and 2013 partners in Indianapolis united to create the 8.1-mile "urban multi-use trail and linear park" in the heart of the city. This effort was led by a nonprofit that engaged and partnered with the city. Together they funded the $63-million project, combining both philanthropic and government dollars including a $25 million federal transportation department grant.

Private Development on Private Lands

These are projects where a private organization takes on all, or almost all, of the project leadership, financial responsibility, and ownership. Although it's highly unlikely that a grand loop trail will ever be privately developed, there are several great examples of smaller loop trails developed by private owners or individuals that have become community walking destinations. The Anchorage Trail in Louisville, Kentucky, and the Anne Springs Close Greenway in Fort Mill, South Carolina, are examples. The Anchorage Trail, the brainchild of pizza magnate "Papa John" Schnatter, is a 2.5-mile trail system with a loop and possibilities to enjoy longer walks by combining the trails on the Schnatter lands with routes along the sidewalks through the adjacent neighborhoods.

Interestingly, this trail lies close to the proposed route of the 100-mile Louisville Loop.

Fort Mill, South Carolina, is a community of 22,000 on the outer edges of Charlotte. The Anne Springs Close Greenway includes more than 36 miles of loop trails on a 2,100-acre private parcel. Some are multiuse hike/bike trails, others are pedestrian only, and there are equestrian pathways. Although it's called a greenway, Chuck Flink, the author of the plan, says that it "does not fit the classic description of a 'greenway.'" He suggests, rather, that it is a "rectangular-shaped environmental and cultural park rather than the long, skinny, linear park associated with American greenways." In his book *The Greenway Imperative*, Chuck suggests that the donors, particularly Anne Springs Close, had conservation in their genes. Ms. Close, he said, was also inspired by her German childhood au pair, "who raised her in accordance with . . . an appreciation of her native ecosystems and included daily hikes through the countryside." As evidenced by her project, she also valued public service, opening her property for all to enjoy. I'm confident that people like Anne Springs Close and John Schnatter can be found in just about any community. Interestingly the Anne Springs Close Greenway is on the Charlotte metro edge. Could it one day be part of a greater Charlotte grand loop?[2]

In addition to these intentional public trails built on private lands, there are great walking opportunities in cemeteries. Many of the larger ones just about everywhere are open to the public free of charge and offer wonderful, pleasant strolling opportunities, such as the Mount Auburn Cemetery in Cambridge, Massachusetts, and the Greenwood Cemetery in Brooklyn, New York. Also, there may some value in incorporating cemeteries into larger loop walks. Having negotiated a couple of trails along the edges of cemeteries, I know it could be worth talking with the owners and operators to see whether there are compatible ways to do that. The key is to ensure that gravesites and mourners are not disturbed. There also may be opportunities to exchange benefits through partnerships to maintain the landscapes next to the trail and possibly memorial donations or plaques commemorating loved ones who have donated to trails.

No Central Authority but Catalytically Inspired and Expanding

In this model there is no single authority, and the big picture is revealed a step at a time. The catalytic approach involves promoting and building smaller projects that inspire and create the will to connect them into bigger systems or networks. This may be a concerted intention, or it may evolve because one successful project is built and the idea catches on.

This happened with Denver's Platte River Greenway. With no central authority, it expanded into a larger regional multicity network. When the Denver Greenway trail was completed through Denver proper in the 1970s, the other communities along the river saw this going on and then initiated and built their own segments of the greenway. Neighboring cities looked at the tributary creeks connecting to the Platte and joined in. Eventually a metro-wide interconnected system of hundreds of miles evolved. There was no single group in charge, although a statewide trail funding program offered motivation. In some ways the proposed grand loop trail around Denver is also taking shape this way, with no detailed plan or authority. Instead, the individual jurisdictions are connecting segments together. Maybe it's intentional, maybe not, but you can now walk a big chunk of the loop envisioned in the concept plan.

Permanence: Have A Strategy for Long-Term Stewardship and Continuity

Think about permanence. This is a multigenerational endeavor. Once the projects are built, we want to be sure they stay in good condition and the values that led to making the improvements are preserved. This includes ensuring that the trails and walks are kept in good repair, that there is a solid, adequately funded and well-managed maintenance program, and that the conservation, scenic, and urban shaping characteristics of the corridors are preserved. This involves having stewardship guidelines built into the planning process and sustaining an ongoing leadership and advocacy organization after the built projects are completed. In some instances, an ownership entity such as a parks department does this. If there's a nonprofit involved, it may stay on board in the role of oversight. Note that sometimes when the physical projects are built, the organizations may fade, losing their sense of mission, or fold. Others shift to a long-term stewardship role. The Appalachian Conservancy, the Pacific Crest Trail Association, and the Bruce Trail Conservancy are good examples of long-term stewardship organizations that actively go on after the trail has been built. Long-term stewardship could be helped by the creation of an endowment through a major grant, bequest, or planned giving program.

Returning to the examples of Olmsted's parkways and, later, greenways, we can see how, through proactive community endeavors, these previously unknown and unheard-of concepts transformed cities for the better. We saw how, over a few decades, these concepts caught on and spread, reshaping cites around the world. Part of what enabled this global proliferation was that the idea was first tried somewhere, it succeeded, and then other places embraced the examples. They were given the vision and the tools and pursued their own green places. This is the expanding, replicating aspect of an easy-to-comprehend, doable concept that meets intrinsic needs.

As more projects are built, the grand loops and town walks vision should offer the same opportunities, becoming a next green step, combining the ideas of Olmsted's parkways and the greenway movement in continuing to make our cities and countrysides more accessible and more welcoming.

Enabling Trail Users

Once our trails and walking routes are built, we want people hiking and walking on them, not just occasionally but regularly. This means encouraging and enabling a broad array of people from diverse backgrounds and perspectives, including potential users who typically do not walk, run, or hike at all. Of course, not everyone will participate, not even a majority, but is it is important to build a critical mass of regular users to ensure continuing support and enthusiasm among public officials, business leaders, and the news media. When successful pilot projects are completed and used, they will demonstrate a demand and, hopefully, make the case for continued investment. Expanding participation starts with first understanding people's core motivations for walking and hiking as well as understanding the impediments and disincentives that keep a significant part of the population from engaging.

Getting People to Routinely Use the Trails

The Walk, Bike, Fit Plan for Commerce City, Colorado, has town walks and grand loops concepts at its core. In the preparation of that plan, there was a dilemma. Multiple trails and sidewalk routes were recommended to improve the city's pedestrian networks. The designers drew great maps and color renderings of happy people out walking and hiking, but there was an elephant in the room: Would a large segment of the population use them regularly? The prime sponsor of the plan, Tri-Countries Health, a public wellness partnership, had the goal of overcoming rampant obesity, improving cardiovascular health, and achieving community fitness by promoting routine physical activity, ideally 30 minutes a day. The objective was not only to create high-quality walking and biking infrastructure but also to enable and encourage people to use them. What was the value of the plan if a significant proportion of the community did not engage? Commerce City has diverse demographics, including working-class enclaves as well as upper-middle-class, affluent neighborhoods, and there are multiple racial and ethnic groups. Promoting broad enthusiasm and usage was no slam-dunk. From this experience it became clear that, not only in Commerce City but just about everywhere, there is no single profile of the citizenry. Indeed, we are increasingly becoming a varied, even fractious society. So how do we win people over?

Fortunately, there are strategies for addressing diverse markets to find common ground and figuring out how to package, brand, and broaden the market for our projects.

Who Will Do It and How Many?

Let's start by looking at the good news. According to the US Bureau of Labor Statistics, walking is the single most popular form of outdoor recreation activity. Running and hiking also rank in the top seventeen sports and exercise activities in the United States. The bad news is that only 18 percent of the population participate in those activities on a typical day.[3] Even more discouraging is that fact that, according to the Outdoor Industry Association, half of the US population does not participate in outdoor recreation despite the proven, positive outcomes. They reported that, sadly, youth participation was declining at rates nearing 5 percent per year.[4]

Motivation Is Tricky Business

In an article titled "Motivation for Exercise," fitness trainer Paige Waehner lists some of the challenges of exercise motivation, including sedentary jobs and lifestyles, being overweight, being too busy or stressed, and people feeling they don't have access to "workout facilities" such as gyms. She also mentions concerns about neighborhood safety. She goes on to compare extrinsic driving forces such as "you should do this so you can look good and be healthy" with intrinsic driving forces such as "because it feels good" and "I love that runner's high."[5] Put another way, we want to understand how immediate, intrinsic rewards are the driving factor. A study published in *Medicine and Science in Sports and Exercise* *found that* "internal motivators like self-efficacy, interest in what they were doing, and enjoyment of exercise had the most success at long-term weight management."[6] In other words, it's not about things people are told they should do but about what they like to do.

For some, encouragement and enabling means a meet-up group, buddy system, or just one friend encouraging another to help them get over the wall of whatever is stopping them. An article in *Texas Monthly* highlighted the notion of friends motivating friends with meet-ups and organized fun outings. Calling themselves the "Hot Girls," a group in Dallas regularly gathers to go out on a walk, often rewarding themselves with margaritas at the completion of their urban trek.[7]

Does Anybody Walk in Eggertsville?

Further exploring this question is an intriguing paper by three urban design researchers at the University at Buffalo School of Architecture and Urban Design. One of the authors, Hiroaki (Hiro) Hata, became very interested in what motivates people to walk.

In pursuit of this question, Hiro joined Daniel Hess and Ernest Sternberg in a study of Eggertsville, an older Buffalo suburb located near the university. They wanted to get a better handle on the principles that can best guide urban designers in promoting urban vitality and better communities, particularly by getting more people walking and having more walkable places that enable and motivate walking. In 2013 they published "Pathways and Artifacts: Neighborhood Design for Physical Activity," which offers significant insight.[8]

Eggertsville is a mid-twentieth-century bungalow community with a traditional grid layout, mostly single-family homes and tree-lined sidewalks. There are convenience stores, other shopping, and a light rail stop nearby. In many ways, Eggertsville's layout conforms with "New Urbanist" principles, which promote connectivity, mixed use, smart transportation, sustainability, and quality of life.[9] But although the community seemed to have all the walkable characteristics, Hess, Hata, and Sternberg observed that people weren't walking. Why not?

The authors observed that more appealing walking infrastructure was needed.[10] They observe that "a variety of destinations, interesting routes, shade and benches, safety and easy access to parks and pathways as well as connectivity were predictors of more walking."[11]

They wrap up their context assessment by offering three lessons: Traditional sidewalks are not enough for today's demands, motivation to walk is at least partly about an engaging and authentic outdoor realm, and traditional parks no longer function the same way. "Although a city park still has a role in providing organized sports such as basketball or baseball, its main use is now the same as that of . . . streets: as the location of pathways conducive to dog-walking, jogging, skate-boarding, therapeutic walking and strolling." They suggest that from a neighborhood perspective there is also a need to bring "*green pathways* through the streets" and that ultimately "every street is served by a pathway, which interconnects to every other pathway [creating] . . . networks of rich recreational opportunities. Town walks and a green overlay would address this need."[12]

They suggest having 16-foot-wide center medians and landscaped walks along with pedestrian-friendly treatments of intersections and crossings. They cite the importance of giving intersections a sense of place with streetscape enhancements and emphasize that pathways should "lead to *artifacts*, built or preserved objects that offer destination and imbue meaning to a walk."[13]

I found their notion of artifacts particularly intriguing when it comes to attracting and motivating users. The goal is to provide authentic meaning through a cultural icon such as a church steeple or a tulip bed or a natural feature such as a tree or bend in a stream.[14] Maybe it's a street sculpture or a nice bench with a view. They expand the notion to describe the values of scripting in features such as more interesting intersections and undulations in the layout to create nooks.

The point they make about engaging people by having destinations and points of interest as a reward, not contrived but worked into the journey, is intriguing. The route becomes a story with subplots along the way.

Getting People out to the Edge on a Grand Loop: Who Wants to Walk around a City?

With the Eggertsville study providing a rich, well-researched investigation of walking in town, can we formulate a similar picture when it comes to grand loop trails? Although I did not find a body of investigation on this, I believe we can glean some intuitive notions about attracting grand loop trail users from the Eggertsville study. Like the proposed pathways in Eggertsville, grand loops are about the experience, enjoyment, and solace with a pinch of fitness thrown in. Perhaps "artifacts" in the form of highlighted attractions along the way can enhance the experience and draw more people. Maybe it's framing an iconic view or a rest area that is also a sculptural element.

Overcoming Myths, Fears, and Not Feeling Welcome

An important part of getting more people out there is to overcome the disincentives that keep many people at home. Fears, some justified and some overblown, inhibit people from hiking and walking not only in the woods but also just outside their front doors. These include anxieties about dangerous, different, or "unusual" people, being accosted or assaulted, being sexually harassed, getting lost, having a medical emergency, hostile dogs, and, of course, traffic hazards. Some of these may be more of a concern to many women who feel more vulnerable and minority groups not feeling safe or welcomed in places.

Fear of Nature

In addressing this question, I interviewed Jamie Siebrase, an outdoors writer authoring articles and books focused on enabling and encouraging trail access and enjoyment. Jamie is also the author of the book *Mythbusting the Great Outdoors.* In our conversations Jamie said, "Many of the people I know who don't regularly participate in the outdoors talk about fears of the unknown." Highlighting bears and weather as common fears, she suggests perspective and preparedness. "Bears are the people of the forest . . . and [if] we can understand their social system and cues it can go a long way toward making the encounter benign." And with weather, she told me, "We can prepare, check forecasts, dress properly and have a contingency plan to find shelter. Some of these, like dealing with a bear, boil down to learning techniques to back away and discourage animal attacks. We can also plan and design to minimize risks," she said.

As Jamie suggests about hiking-in-the-woods anxieties, we can look at those concerns and get out messages that debunk the misinformation and give people tools to put things in their proper statistical perspective. For trail hiking, the annual fatality rate is low: 1 in 15,000.[15] For a pedestrian in town, the US National Safety Council Injury Facts table of preventable death states the odds of dying in a lifetime is 1 in 553. Compare these numbers to the lifetime numbers of 1 in 6 for heart disease and the odds of dying in a motor vehicle crash, 1 in 101.[16] There are risks in going on a hike or taking a walk around town, but, according to the statistics, the hazards are not remarkable, especially compared to staying on the couch or leaving home only in an automobile.[17]

Planners can work on both designing and managing to reduce risks and to reduce the perception of risk. Part of this is getting the word out, that when it comes to overall risks in life, walking or hiking regularly is a better choice than being sedentary, considering that the risks of heart disease or diabetes are many times higher.[18]

Fear of Isolated Trails

For Julie George, the runner whose story appears at the start of chapter 2, running is also a social engagement, and she prefers to run with others, not only for companionship but also for safety reasons. I asked about her thoughts on safety along grand loops, and she said, "As a woman, I prefer not to run in the dark or alone if it feels remote. There is a need to feel safe. Are there enough feet, eyes, people?"

According to *Streetsblog USA*, a Columbia University survey found that 30 percent of women queried "always" or "very frequently chose other modes . . . or skip" walking because they feel unsafe. The study also found that "70% of the women surveyed listed the possibility of sexual assault as their number one worry."[19]

Although there will always be concerns that inhibit some people from getting out there, we do have the opportunity to overcome many of the real and perceived issues by carefully envisioning, planning, designing, and managing the projects we build. Plan trails and walks with safety and security (and the perception of safety and security) in mind and publicize the successes. Show, with improvements and branding, that they offer a safer and more enjoyable alternative to what was there before. To promote trail safety, the Rails-to-Trails Conservancy suggests that trail design should eliminate overgrown vegetation and tall shrubs in order to minimize hiding places along the trail, maintain long sight lines for users, and include security lighting at trailheads and in parking lots. Emergency phones or call boxes and emergency vehicle access are also useful tools for some trails.[20]

"You Don't Belong Here"

Charles Brown, a transportation expert at Rutgers University who focuses on "arrested mobility," expressed in an interview how profoundly people who don't meet the "white stereotype" are affected, especially in backcountry places. "You can feel vulnerable and exposed," he said.

Amanda Machado, in a 2020 *Sierra* article, points out that Oregon, well known for its outdoor destinations, once wrote the exclusion of Black people directly into its constitution. Today, of course, thankfully, Oregon is one of the more progressive and tolerant states. Sadly, two other states, Idaho and Montana, also outdoors and hiking destinations, report the highest rates of hate crimes. When describing the unfriendly looks she received while traveling through small towns on a camping trip, Machado writes, "In so many ways, any person of color in the United States who loves hiking and camping is used to this. We have always known that in order to access the most beautiful corners of the United States, you must first pass through some of its most racist corners."[21]

Sadly, there is no simple solution, says Charles Brown, but traveling in groups can help. He recommends working with minority outdoors organizations, such as Blackpackers, which provides resources, gear, and career opportunities to open the outdoors for more people of color, and suggests the option of going on group trips, such as a church or school expedition.[22,23] Clearly, in our planning and messaging we need to convey the notion of inclusion and tolerance. This could include posting a welcoming message on entry signs at trailheads and ensuring that potential users can see people they identify with in brochures and other trail and walk literature. The safety planning measures detailed in the section above are also applicable to this issue.

Drawing In Those Who Would if They Could and Those Who Just Don't

In addition to the question of fears, there are other considerations when we think about enabling and encouraging hiking and walking. Based on research and personal observation, listed below are several types of groups to consider when we think about who would and who wouldn't be likely to use the trails and walking routes we build. There are those who feel constrained for various reasons, including ability, economic constraints, lack of time, and lack of interest.

Do I Have the Ability?

One of my neighbors used to be a runner. Then he wasn't. The last time that I ran into him, he was walking. He told me about the mountain biking accident injuries. Then there was a back surgery followed by other neuromuscular problems. Finally, he suffered a mysterious eye infection, severely compromising his eyesight. He said, "At first I got pretty discouraged" and sat at home. Yet there he was, not only walking but regularly taking 3-plus-mile hikes and feeling much better by doing it. He created his own doorstep loops, including the route where I passed him on my routine walks.

Many people might want to walk but for a physical or emotional reason don't. According to the Centers for Disease Control and Prevention, this group includes one in four people in the United States. And that's just the numbers of what we might call "clinical" challenges such as difficulty with mobility, sight, hearing, and cognitive issues.[24]

In addition, there are people who use a wheelchair or a walking assistance device or have pain or mobility difficulties due to joint injuries, balance problems, eyesight or hearing difficulties, or cardiovascular or pulmonary problems. Others are able but may be discouraged or embarrassed to be seen exercising because of their body shape, gait, or other appearance feature that makes them feel uncomfortable in public. In each of these instances, we want to look at ways to motivate, encourage, and engage those who, with the right encouragement, might feel more confident and comfortable getting out there.

Having high-quality, accessible places to walk or hike certainly helps. The community, where I live and routinely walk, has these amenities by design. Pursuing grand loops and town walks can help make them common.

The process also includes reaching out to these groups in a frank and understanding manner aimed at solutions and encouragement. Planners and advocates can also make a practice of depicting people of various sizes, shapes, and abilities on the trails and walks in plan reports, illustrations, brochures, and videos. There can be links on project websites to sources that directly address potential barriers such as weight, fitness, and joint problems when considering a walk. It may include testimonials by those who, despite challenges, got out there, how they did it, and the rewards they reaped. Parks agencies can engage by working with orthopedic centers, physical therapists, and other medical practitioners to get grand loops and town walks on their menus of rehabilitation regimens. Planning measures for accessibility detailed in chapter 4 also will enable more people to use the trails.

I'm Too Old

By 2050, a sixth of the population will be over age 65.[25] However, "too old" is a pervasive misperception. There is no question that age brings with it many challenges, ranging from sore joints to impaired mental capacity.

But planners can help the anticipate needs of some seniors with amenities such as clear wayfinding, easier terrain, and more benches and toilet facilities.

I Can't Afford That

As mentioned in chapter 1, a key objective of creating grand loops and town walks is to reach out to groups who do not have access to a car or gas money or otherwise feel left out or limited by tight personal financial conditions. We want to get the message out that there is an affordable option for them and that they should feel welcomed. Wherever possible, town walk routes should be within walking distance of neighborhoods or accessible by public transit.

It may be helpful to work with the local public transit agency to identify key gateway points along bus and transit lines, clearly marked and branded, that lead to attractive routes. Portland, Oregon, marks parks on its regional transit maps. In fact, Portland also offers its 4-T (Trail, Tram, Trolley, and Train) program, which boasts a place "where a trail, a tram, and a train combine for a one-of-a-kind, multi-modal way to enjoy Portland . . . one of the nation's most walkable cities."[26] Seattle, New York, Denver, and Vancouver have similarly pursued the notion of "car-free hikes."[27] Seattle has its Greater King County Trailhead Direct program, where trail and transit access information is integrated and available online.

An offshoot of this easy access concept is a transit-to-trails program. These are programs that connect trails to bus or train stops, typically at the end of the line. In some instances, a special shuttle van is there to carry a hiker directly to a trailhead. These stops could become trail transit hubs located strategically along a loop. A hiker could take the transit to one hub, maybe hike to another hub, and catch a train or bus back home. Branding, discount passes, or tokens could be motivating.

Another encouraging note in this process is efforts by lawmakers to build a national program. In 2021, congressman Jimmy Gomez and senator Cory Booker introduced the Transit to Trails Act "to create a grant program to fund projects that make transportation to green spaces and public lands more accessible to critically underserved communities."[28]

In some places online rideshare services have offered discount promotions. Jefferson County Open Space, near Denver, launched a pilot program in cooperation with Lyft to get hikers to its edge-of-town mountain park trailheads. Done in part to reduce overcrowding at trailhead parking lots, the program can be a great help for people without cars.[29]

Schools are potential partners, organizing class trips to hike on a loop both in town and on the edge of town. Some might even be overnight outings where camping is facilitated in existing or "staged" campsites.

I Have Kids

Some parents may feel constrained by competing time demands, school commitments, sports team practices and games, and kids' abilities or interest in trail activities. We can also look at young people under the driving age, who can't readily access many places to hike and walk on their own. Jamie Siebrase, who also wrote a book about hiking with kids, *Hiking with Kids Colorado*, identifies transportation and time as two of the biggest barriers. Close-in and reasonably predictable routes, as well as child-friendly amenities including rest spots, points of interest to children, and "pocket" play areas, can be big incentives.[30]

It can be helpful to include families with children in the planning process. When planning a trail system, my colleagues and I have invited parents to bring their kids to public meetings. We gave them markers and newsprint pads and asked them to draw up and present what they thought we should do.

It's Just Not What We Do

For some people, trails, walking, and physical activity are just not part of their culture. They're just not interested. They may say "I'm not capable" or even that it's demeaning. There may be an ingrained impression that the well-to-do ride and the poor walk. Some folks just don't want a lifestyle change. It might be helpful to reach out to this group in a friendly, noncritical way. Tell them about the project. Ask whether they would consider using such a facility and whether there are features that might attract them and motivate them to engage. In some instances, perspectives might change. Getting the message out there about trail and walk projects might strike a chord.

I Don't Have the Time

Many people feel overwhelmed and have great difficulty finding time to commit to daily outdoor activity because of work and family demands. It's a feeling of "If I go out walking, things I need to do won't get done." Better, closer-to-home infrastructure can help. Mark Fenton, a public health, planning, and transportation consultant, suggests promoting a simple incremental program such as combining some walking into necessary trips. It could include promoting walking meetings or the value of going out for a walk to formulate a business idea or find a solution. A town walk could even serve as a walking conference room.

Incentives and Programming

Incentives and programs can help overcome reasons why people don't walk and hike. Here are a few examples.

Insurance and Health Cost Reductions and Employee Prescription Programs

Several leading health and life insurance companies have proactive fitness programs that offer cash-back incentives on premiums for those who engage in a meaningful level of fitness-promoting physical activity. Humana, a health insurance company, offered a program called Go365, an "employee wellness program" tailored to "give a company of any size the ability" to participate in an incentive wellness program that includes "verifiable activities" such as walking.[31]

In another instance, the John Hancock Company, an insurance company, assembled a program called "Vitality" that "rewards healthy living." Policy holders receive discounts on outdoor fitness gear and qualify for up to a 15 percent premium discount by agreeing to walk regularly.

In promoting a project, it is well worth talking with a few insurance executives and health organizations to see what programs they have and whether there are ways to enhance them. It's possible that companies will adopt and maybe even fund a project. The "Medical Mile" in Little Rock, Arkansas, is a great example. Mayor Jim Daley called it "an economic, health, and environmental conservation stimulator." A coalition of hospital groups, physicians, and other providers, along with the Arkansas Department of Health, jumped on board, raising over $2 million to build a "Wellness Promenade" along the Arkansas riverfront.[32]

Programming

Another way to draw people out is to program activities along trails and walking routes. These include organized and guided hikes and walks, races, art exhibits, festivals, summer camps, volunteer stewardship projects, outdoor classrooms, and school outing visits. Indeed, a grand loop or a town walk can be an excellent venue for these types of activities and a great way to draw more people out who otherwise might not visit or even be aware of the trail. Programs can be organized and led by the managing parks agency, an affiliated nonprofit, or independent groups including schools, churches, and service and environmental organizations.

In many cities there are groups that regularly lead walks and hikes both in town and on the city edges. The Wolf River Conservancy in Memphis offers a K–12 youth program with hands-on visits to the Wolf River Greenway and other conservancy lands where kids learn about conservation, biodiversity, wildlife, and other topics.[33] In Denver, the Greenway Foundation, offers ten weeks of summer camp along the Platte River Trail.[34] And for decades the Sierra Club has run an inner-city outing program, now called Inspiring Connections Outdoors, as a way to introduce young people, particularly those of limited means, to the outdoors.[35] Imagine a hundred-mile-long grand loop trail as an overnight summer camp venue with hiking, camping, wildlife viewing, and even hands-on stewardship projects. That summer camp wouldn't need a parcel of land. It could consist of a supported trek on a grand loop.

Programming also includes races and other special events. Nothing promotes interest, enthusiasm, and even media exposure like a race or a special event. This might be an organized walk along a town walk or an extreme race competition along a 100-mile grand loop course. It might be a street happening, festival, or maybe a Halloween "haunted trail." As an aside, I recommend that events, especially races, be professionally organized to avoid risks and liability.

Getting the Word Out and Working with Influencers

Getting the word out is a big part of getting people to engage. The process starts with crafting an inspiring message that will enable, encourage, engage, and resonate broadly. Think about the groups, you want target: youth, families, diverse income and ethnicity demographics, locals, and tourists.

Digital Media

If advertising spending is any indication, digital outlets are outpacing the traditional realms of broadcast television, radio, and newspapers.[36] Digital media includes a range of text and video platforms. There are professionals who can help, from digital media marketers to individual bloggers and vloggers (video bloggers).

TravelNevada has marketed a program striving to get people to look beyond the Strip. One of the leading features suggests taking "the very best day trips from Las Vegas," heading out to destinations along the edges of the city that include state parks, a national conservation area, and other iconic places. Several of the destinations described as "where to go beyond the glow" are along the Vegas Valley Rim Trail route.

Juliana Broste is an Emmy Award–winning filmmaker and market strategist who showcases adventures and experiences around the world through video, including the Travel Nevada Neon to Nature program. She is known for her travel and tourism work.[37] When asked about how digital marketing can help promote grand loops and town walk usage, she had several tips. First, define your target audience, thinking about the diverse groups, such as hikers, families, foodies, sports enthusiasts, youth, and seniors, who might be intrigued to visit your trail or walk for various reasons. She likes the video format because "a real person talking out at the site is more authentic and compelling."

She cites YouTube, Twitter, TikTok, Facebook, and Instagram as strong platforms to reach a broad cross-section of the population as well as specific niches. When reaching out to potential sponsors and promoters, she says it's important to clearly define the projects and the benefits to the people who will use the trails as well as the returns on the investment, such as hotel stays and meal purchases.

She says it is also smart to team up with a destination market organization or a local tourism marketing board. These can be membership based or industry or government funded. She says, "Make the case to them to support a campaign."

As more and more people come out to walk, they will patronize restaurants, convenience stores, coffee shops, and lodging. Trails and walking-oriented travel are expanding rapidly worldwide. According to the United Nations World Tourism Organization, "Walking tourism is now one of the most popular ways to experience a destination. It allows tourists to better engage with local people, nature, and culture. It also meets the growing demand of travelers of outdoor activities in general. . . . Walking tourism can be developed anywhere as a sustainable tourism offer with a relatively small investment."[38]

Indeed, the economic aspect has spawned a new movement called Trail Towns where communities proactively pursue trail projects. As trail advocate Jan Hancock, who is working on a trail that will connect the Phoenix grand loop to Las Vegas grand loop, put it, "This is a 'credit card' urban-focused tourism-based trail system. Bring your credit card and enjoy the hospitality, businesses, and destinations in the communities along the trail."[39]

Coupon programs with service or goods providers such as hotels, restaurants, and sports apparel companies are another promotional tool.

Traditional Media

Check the travel, environmental, and lifestyle features and sports sections of newspapers and monitor television and radio to identify writers who specialize in outdoor recreation and tourism. Hiring a public relations agency can be helpful here too. Assemble a media contact list and write a clear, concise press release. This may be particularly effective around events such as groundbreakings or visual action items such as craning in a new footbridge.

Free Media Coverage

Earned free media can be a place to look before investing in a media campaign. A compelling press release can get you on the news locally or even nationally. Juliana also suggests inviting people in the hospitality profession, influencers, and members of both the digital and traditional media to launch events such as a master plan presentation or groundbreaking. A high-quality photo and video library will allow media outlets to run the story if they can't afford to send a reporter or photographer.

Working with Content Creators

Great storytelling can bring the trail experience to life. Some content creators speak to specific audiences such as families, couples, and solo travelers. Others focus on price points such as budget or luxury travel or interests such as outdoors, food, spa, and business travel. Some are funded by ad dollars for visits to their posts, and other are funded through direct commissions.

Feature Stories

Once a project is built or even partially completed, a travel feature can be a powerful way to get the word out. Perhaps your local tourism entity could be persuaded to invest in a paid feature, or a writer could be recruited to submit a story to the appropriate print, broadcast, or digital media outlets.

Paper Maps and Guidebooks

Paper maps publicize, encourage, and enable. In the field they're easier to read than a flat screen, especially in the sun, and there's no battery involved. Many public parks and open space agencies have them.

We now move on to envision through a series of thought experiments how these trails can work in different places.

CHAPTER 8

Plans, Visions, and Thought Experiments

*"From 30,000 feet you see the blobs that are cites, but you gotta
look at the open spaces that predominate around them.
We need those places!"*

—Jan Hancock, trails writer and advocate

From Phoenix to Louisville to Denver to Jeju, we can see that the grand loop and town walk concepts are workable. The next question is, How replicable are they? Like the greenway vision, can they start in a few places and spread universally? In addressing this question, I looked at several inspiring plans and projects in progress that show the great promise of replicating these ideas widely. To demonstrate diverse settings, I looked at locations with different climates, topography, and cultures to see what might be possible. I considered the challenges as well as the opportunities to expand walkability access and benefit underserved areas. Most of the places had partial trail segments in place or exhibited potential in some way. In building on this exercise, I assembled several thought experiments imagining what could be.

My research started with looking at maps, satellite views, Google Street View, and other remote sensing tools. I turned to many of the existing projects mentioned earlier in this book for inspiration and as enabling examples. In the Maricopa Trail mode of connecting parks with the loop trail, I tried to find existing attractive parks and publicly accessible open spaces and link them together. From an access standpoint, I particularly liked linking destinations such as state parks and regional open spaces, as these tend to be closer in and welcoming places for a broad cross-section of the public. For grand loops I looked for towns, hamlets, and camping areas along the way that could become service nodes. The Google Maps direction tool in the "walking" mode helped significantly. I also reviewed local studies, planning documents, and articles and used them to visualize opportunities and potential. I also shared the ideas with local people in some of the places and was pleased to get favorable, even enthusiastic responses.

A Grand Loop around Dallas–Ft. Worth

"An entire loop of trails around the city . . . (an) integrated Trail Circuit, would mean that there is no end of the line."

—*Dallas Morning News*[1]

One of the fastest-growing regions in North America, the Dallas–Fort Worth metroplex has a population of 7.6 million. Some of the outlying counties have seen nearly a 30 percent increase over the most recent decade.[2] Much of the growth is beyond the city center, which means there is a lot of open area being quickly gobbled up. I had done trail planning on the Johnson Creek Greenway that runs through Arlington, between Dallas and Ft. Worth, and walked that route. So, I had a sense of the climate and the Texas prairie landscape. I also knew from that experience that there is trail enthusiasm both among the citizens and leaders. I wondered whether a grand loop could work there.

Inspired by the Maricopa Trail concept of linking large open space parks on the edges of the metro area, I took a similar approach for a loop around greater Dallas–Ft. Worth. It turns out there are several significant state parks on the edges of this metro area. I also looked for outlying towns and other settlements along a potential route where a trekker could stop for a meal or spend the night. The metro area has a number of these communities, spaced along a potential loop route between the state parks. Many of these communities have points of historic and cultural interest, including local museums and other important features such as the route of the historic Chisholm Trail, famed for the cattle drives of the 1800s. I found Google Maps particularly useful because it shows terrain, vegetation, points of interest, and networks of backroads that have potential to double as on-street walking (or biking) routes. Of course, the Google Maps street view proved priceless when I wanted to get an on-the-ground view of the landscape.

At first, as I looked at the sprawling area on a map and glanced at what appeared to be some very stark, flat landscapes, I was discouraged. With the heat and humidity in summer, out in the open exposed to heat, wind, and storms, who'd want to walk there? Ranchers and others dwelling along the edges might not take kindly to hikers passing through. I wondered about securing rights of way. Were there enough walkable backroads with safe places to walk without hordes of cars and trucks whizzing by? As I looked at more maps, I became more encouraged.

The emerging plans from the North Central Texas Council of Governments for a 2045 Veloweb that would form an interconnected system of hike/bike path loops overlaying the entire urbanized area added to my enthusiasm. According to the council, this would expand the existing 775 miles of trails, as of 2022, into a "1728-mile network of pathways serving 12 counties and over 115 cities—an interstate for bicyclists and pedestrians."[3] In a way, the Veloweb is a step beyond greenways, because it will evolve from linear routes to loops woven into regional networks. Although this vision would work wonders for the livability of the Dallas–Ft. Worth region, it is primarily an urban bike path system, although pedestrians are not excluded. So I decided to look at the urban–rural edges to see where there is the potential for walkable routes and where the locals might be welcoming.

I found a story by Cameron Dodd in *Texas Parks and Wildlife Magazine* titled "Lone Star Walkabout: A Hiker Sets Off to Be the First to Walk the 130-Mile Northeast Texas Trail."[4] Dodd writes, "With sore knees, wet feet, and the beginnings of blisters on my soles, I follow the trail into town, where I'm planning to camp. Storm clouds continue to form overhead, and I'm eager to set up camp for the night. Just as I begin unpacking my tent, a man from a nearby house walks over. I assume he's going to chase me off, but to my surprise he greets me cheerfully and . . . introduces himself as Harold and explains that . . . he knows all about the trail. He tells me there's a store open until 8, and an old rodeo arena . . . where I'll find better shelter for my tent." Harold then gets Cameron "a better walking stick," and later he enjoys beers at a cabin of one of the locals before setting out again. This story certainly helped assuage my concerns about "desolation" and encouraged me that there can be a sense of welcoming in these rural areas—two important considerations in determining the walkability of a route.

Although it is not yet part of a grand loop around Dallas–Ft. Worth, the Northeast Texas Trail seems to enable the concept. It suggests the potential, and an example of community acceptance for a rural walking route though the abandoned rail line certainly enabled securing a right of way. Maybe the example, not to mention the potential local economic benefits, will encourage others around the edges of Dallas–Ft. Worth to agree to granting rights of way. Combined with the Veloweb, it's not hard to envision a grand loop out on the edges of the metroplex with many subloops and connections to population centers. Time of year and time of day would factor into when it is best to walk these prairie-like spaces, but the possibilities of a pleasant, rewarding walk are there. Strategically placed shelters, shade spots, or waystations (trail depots) (described in chapter 4) could help. Indeed, in the face of sprawling growth, a grand loop coupled with open space and rural landscape conservation programs could potentially better shape the future the Dallas–Ft. Worth region.

In plotting my imaginary grand loop, I decided to start at the western terminus of the Northeast Texas Trail in the rural town of Farmersville, a community of about 3,600 residents about 45 miles from downtown Dallas. From here the route heads west across Texas prairie lands to Roy Roberts (Lake) State Park, with its beaches and campsites. The path then curves to the southwest, connecting to scenic Lake Mineral Wells State Park, which also offers swimming and camping. Next the trek heads southeast to Lake Claiborne State Park, with its wooded nature trails, beaches, and camping. All along the way between these scenic lakes there are towns and hamlets with services and points of interest including museums and monuments that highlight the local culture and recall the history of this part of Texas. The trail would then wrap around the east side of the metroplex area, connecting to Lake Tawakoni State Park and then rejoining the Northeast Texas Trail at the hamlet of Floyd. From Floyd hikers would again head west back to Farmersville, experiencing a 10-mile segment of the rail trail. The total route could be 400 to 450 miles or longer and could weave along country roads and future connecting trails as the grand loop develops over time (figure 8.1).

The Toronto Vision: Greenbelts Forming a Grand Loop Trail

Metropolitan Toronto has a population of 6.3 million.[5] It's the eighth largest metro area in North America, with 7.7 million people projected

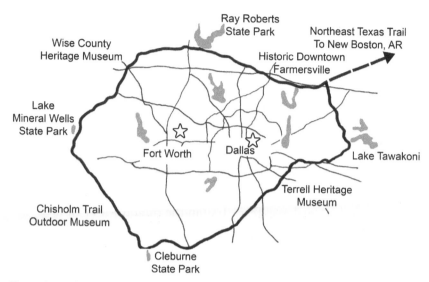

Figure 8.1. Dallas–Ft. Worth grand loop concept. (Credit: Bill Neumann)

by 2025. Unlike most North American cities, significant portions of the lands in the greater Toronto remain in dedicated open spaces including forests, farmland, and preserves, such as the Rouge Urban National Park, which flanks the eastern border of the city.

In 2005, recognizing the value of these green spaces and the increasing pressures of Toronto's explosive growth, the Ontario provincial government passed the Greenbelt Act, identifying a 1.8-million-acre greenbelt forming the edge of an area that includes Toronto proper and adjacent cities along the western edge of Lake Ontario. In addition to protecting agricultural lands, forests, animals, and plant communities, the greenbelt program provides Torontonians "access to parks, hiking trails, rivers, lakes and other recreational lands." The program also stipulates the preservation of "many historic communities, villages, towns, and hamlets . . . promoting . . . education about the region's cultural heritage."[6] One key benefit of grand loops is urban shaping, including promoting greenbelts such as Toronto's. Given the Metro Toronto regional land use and open space conservation context, imagining a grand loop was a significantly easier and encouraging task. Toronto has a strong trail and open space program with a lot of the infrastructure in place to form a grand loop and demonstrates what a grand loop could add in an area that already has policies like the Greenbelt Act and many parks and greenways. This is not to say Toronto is perfect, but it is an inspiring model for other metro areas to emulate in terms of both visionary policies like the Greenbelt Act and the execution of an ambitious trail network plan.

A Toronto grand loop could start where the Rouge River Trail meets Lake Ontario and move west along the Waterfront Trail. This segment passes through the attractive and intensely urbanized Toronto lakeshore. The route could then turn northwest at the Etobicoke Greenway in Mississauga and form the west side of the loop. The Oak Ridges Trail could then form the northern edge of the loop before turning south to pass through Rouge Urban National Park, forming the eastern edge before connecting back to the shores of Lake Ontario. The imagined grand loop would be a 150- to 200-mile trekking route, with most of it 20 to 35 miles from downtown Toronto (figure 8.2). It is noteworthy that substantial portions of this possible grand loop run through Toronto greenbelt lands or other designated significant landscapes, including the Niagara Escarpment. A grand loop would link these spaces together and form a necklace of landscapes around metro Toronto. By extending the loop a bit further southwest, the Toronto grand loop could link to the Bruce Trail, an iconic route that runs 550 miles from Niagara Falls to the shores of Lake Huron.[7] Like the Northeast Texas Trail, the Bruce Trail would be an adjunct to a possible Toronto grand loop. The loop would also connect to the coast-to-coast Canada Trail that passes through the city.[8]

Besides accessing and revealing some of greater Toronto's best natural features, this potential route is optimal in that it connects numerous cities, towns, villages, and hamlets along the city's outskirts and accesses downtown Toronto and iconic features such as Toronto Island and the

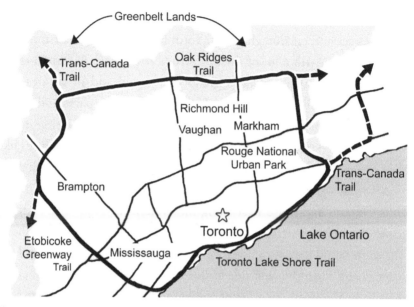

Figure 8.2. Toronto grand loop concept. (Credit: Bill Neumann)

CN Tower. With many accessible places to dine and lodge, it could be a potential daypack route. In addition, and in furtherance of the transit-to-trails concept, much of the route could be readily accessible via transit lines, including from Toronto's airports. With many segments already in place, one could make most of this trek today, but forming it into a grand loop would add important elements such as cohesiveness, safety, and accessibility, leading to broader use and contributing to urban shaping. Although it wasn't intended as such, it is possible to download the maps in the 2019 *Trail Strategy Report for the Greater Toronto Region* and plan a trek![9]

An Amazing Grand Loop around Buffalo, New York

If you follow the Bruce Trail south from Toronto, after a four- to five-day hike you'll reach the Niagara River and the US border. Unlike

Toronto or Dallas–Ft. Worth, Buffalo, New York, with a metro area population of 1.1 million,[10] is not a burgeoning urban destination. It was a fading Rust Belt city, although it is beginning to recover and reinvent itself. Back in its heyday, it was an industrial hub. With economic prosperity came philanthropy and cultural benefits including a world-class art gallery, a philharmonic orchestra, and a science museum. These trends also fostered iconic architectural examples and urban planning with the works of Louis Sullivan, Frank Lloyd Wright, and Frederick Law Olmsted shaping the city. It was in Buffalo that Olmsted, in the latter half of the twentieth century, laid out a pioneering masterplan that envisioned an interconnected network of parks and tree-lined parkways. When arriving in Buffalo, Olmsted called it the "best planned city . . . in North America if not the World."[11]

After World War II and into the 1970s Buffalo began to decline, led by the downsizing of the steel mills and other deindustrialization. Businesses failed, people were out of work, and many homes became vacant. Sadly, as was the trend in many urban areas in the late twentieth century, boosters and civic leaders built a freeway along the city's river and lakeshore edges, all but isolating the populace from the region's major water features. Things got so bleak that, in the late 1970s Mark Margolis, a local graphic artist, coined the unflattering moniker "Buffalo: The City of No Illusions." Nonetheless, the region managed to hold on to many of its better features, including the Olmsted parks and parkways and exceptional bucolic landscapes along the outer edges of a compact city.

In more recent decades Buffalo's recovery began with the development of a major university complex, the establishment of leading medical treatment and research centers, and the repurposing of old industrial buildings to house lofts, new businesses, and restaurants. Significantly, the former steel mill lands that extend along the lakeshore just south of the city were largely cleared and cleaned up. Now this area hosts the

Tift Nature Preserve, a major conservation and birding destination, and Buffalo Harbor State Park.

Looking a few miles farther out to the edges the Buffalo metroplex, there are several other significant, even iconic landscape features. To the south there is scenic Cattaraugus Creek and the iconic Zoar Valley Multiple Use Area. To the east, there are rural landscapes with farmlands and hamlets, and on the north there is the dramatic Niagara Escarpment that overlooks flatlands extending to Lake Ontario.

Although Buffalo does not have as ambitious an open space, trails, and greenbelt plan as Toronto's, there are existing trails and planned projects that could lead to a world-class grand loop belt (figure 8.3). Starting near Niagara Falls, a world tourism destination approximately 25 miles north of Buffalo, a grand loop route could follow the Shoreline Trail along the Niagara River from Youngstown on Lake Ontario to Lake Erie near downtown Buffalo. It would connect a string of parks, cultural centers, and the iconic Niagara Falls along its length. There could be a parallel trail on the Canadian side following the Niagara River Parkway from the town of Niagara-on-the-Lake, with its wineries and boutique hotels, to historic Fort Erie.[12] From downtown Buffalo the route would continue along the proposed Shoreline Trail, following Lake Erie to Evangola State Park near the mouth of Cattaraugus Creek.[13]

The loop route then could turn east and follow a potential greenway through the Zoar Valley Multiuse Area, with its cliffs and wooded bottomlands and then continue to the town of Sardinia. A network of rural roads holds promise to provide suitable connections. From there, the loop could turn north, running through mostly rural country toward Gasport, a historic stop along the Erie Canal. Numerous backroads and rail lines with trail conversion potential could facilitate this segment. At Gasport, there are several options to close the loop back to the Niagara River. One is to follow the existing Erie Canal Trail to Lockport and link to Lewiston via rural roads or a future trail. Alternatively, the

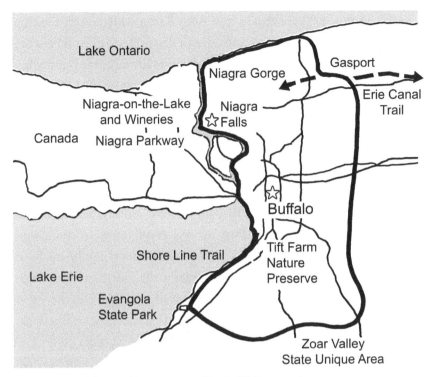

Figure 8.3. Buffalo grand loop concept. (Credit: Bill Neumann)

route could head further north, following the Somerset Rail Trail to the Lake Ontario shore. It would then head west along an already proposed extension of the Shoreline Trail to Youngstown and to back to Niagara Falls.[14] This would complete a striking 170- to 200-mile route roughly around the rim of Erie County, with options for portions through Canada with links to the Bruce Trail.

We Live Where You Vacation: Loops around Sarasota, Florida

In the 1970s, as Buffalo and much of the Rust Belt was suffering from disinvestment, the World War II generation, reaching retirement age, headed south to a warmer climate. Many moved to the southeast Florida coast to Miami, Ft. Lauderdale, and Boca Raton while others took up residence along the Gulf Coast, including a sleepier strip of land between Tampa and Naples. In the decades that followed, Florida's population surged from 6.7 million in 1970 to nearly 22 million in 2021. Florida is now the third most populous state in the United States.[15]

Located approximately an hour south of Tampa, Sarasota is now one of Florida's magnets of growth, with the area population more than tripling from 120,000 to 453,000 during the Florida growth boom.[16] Sarasota has spectacular beaches, a number of sizable state parks and wildlife preserves nearby, and a thriving arts and cultural scene. Storms and summer heat notwithstanding, the region offers a mild climate for outdoor activities much of the year. As a grand loop candidate Sarasota has some hefty challenges, particularly the vast, flat, somewhat featureless inland terrain on the east edge of the city. On the other hand, it has miles of spectacular Gulf of Mexico shoreline on the west, the Manatee River estuary on the north, and the Myakka River and trendy Venice to the south. These two prominent inland water system features, the Manatee and Myakka rivers, form two sides of a potential loop encircling Sarasota. The Gulf Shore forms the third leg, running along the string of keys off the coast. The three legs combine to form a roughly a 140-mile corridor. This potential waterway loop, along with the beaches, offers a palette of the region's major state parks and wildlife preserves. There are thousands of acres of conservation lands, trails, and interpretive sites. These include Lake Manatee State Park, the Duette Preserve, Myakka River State Park, the T. Mabry Carlton, Jr. Memorial Reserve, Deer Prairie Creek Preserve, and the Myakka State Forest. Taken together, these natural spaces suggest not only a route for a trail but an opportunity to form a major greenbelt conservation area the likes of which is happening in Toronto. It could be a blue–green triangle defined by the two rivers and Gulf shoreline forming the third leg. There is tremendous potential!

The Florida Trust for Public Land already has a vision for the Gulf Coast of Florida: a 336-mile trail linking seven counties and serving 21 million people.[17] The Florida Gulf Coast Trail, envisioned to extend from south of Naples to the Tampa area, includes a side loop on the north side of the Sarasota area linking the Gulf shores to the inland Lake Parish preserve areas south of Tampa. I expand on this concept here, enlarging the loop to form more of a complete circle around Sarasota that includes two state conservation areas to the east (figure 8.4).

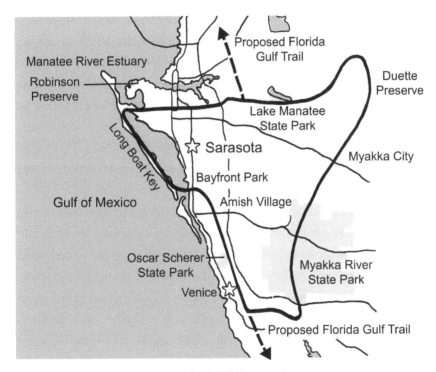

Figure 8.4. Sarasota loops concept. (Credit: Bill Neumann)

If we start at Bayfront Park, on Sarasota Bay near downtown, it is a short distance to the 14-mile Legacy Trail, a rail trail that forms a spine from Sarasota on the north to Venice on the south. This route follows the length of the former track where the Ringling Brothers and Barnum & Bailey Circus, which wintered in Sarasota, staged its famous circus trains.[18] Trekkers could follow the Legacy Trail southward, passing near Oscar Scherer State Park and on to trendy Venice. (In the future there could be a junction here with the Florida Gulf Coast Trail for those wanting to continue toward Naples.) The Sarasota grand loop would turn east at Venice and link to the trail network in Myakka River State Park before continuing on to Myakka City and the Duette Preserve area. The inland parks and preserves feature vast Florida hemlock pine stands, wetland, prairie, and wildlands. Then a connection could be made passing through Lake Manatee State Park to the Manatee River estuary on the north. The route would then follow the proposed loop section of the Florida Gulf Coast Trail across the north edge of Sarasota, returning to the Gulf at the Robinson Preserve. From here the route would follow an existing trail along the length of Long Boat Key, returning to Bayfront Park, crossing Sarasota Bay via the John Ringling Causeway. This would not be an easy project, but building on the Gulf Coast Trail vision and the existing Legacy Trail is worth a look.

Another approach would be to think of this grand loop as a hybrid walking–paddling route. Trekkers could enjoy a combined journey, hiking where there are upland trails and paddling the navigable sections of the rivers and Sarasota Bay between the keys and the mainland. Note that Florida already has a designated blueway paddle trail that follows the entire coast, passing adjacent to Sarasota. Maybe local outfitters could organize trips, conveniently shuttling kayaks to traverse the water parts of the loop.

In a nutshell, the Sarasota area has its challenges in laying out a grand loop system, but opportunities also abound. Segments are in place, and there are potential connecting routes. In a community rich in natural and cultural attractions, the advantages as a tourist destination are exceptional. In a region still in its growth phase, with probably several more major planned communities being built along its eastern hinterland edges, there is a compelling impetus for community leaders and planners to get out ahead of the curve, to dedicate trail routes through the new development and envision the preservation of green spaces and blue spaces. They could create a robust green network by thinking ahead.

Imagining a Town Walk: Uniting Neighborhoods in Washington, DC

There is potential to create town walks in thousands of locations virtually anywhere with streets and sidewalks. There are already successful proof-of-concept examples such as the Turquoise Trail and the 5280 Trail that planners could turn to when advocating for town walks. There are also opportunities to build upon in-progress parks or greenway projects as a starting point, or as hubs, of a town walk loop. The 11th Street Bridge Park in Washington, DC, is particularly interesting because a major goal of the park is establishing connectivity between two areas of Washington separated not only by a river but also by income and demographic differences.[19] A town walk that includes the 11th Street Bridge Park would contribute an expanded green overlay and ideally increase park usage by providing safe and pleasant ways to get to the new Bridge Park.

The Anacostia River separates two major Washington, DC, districts: the Eighth Ward, which includes the Anacostia Neighborhood, and the Sixth Ward, East Hill district of the city. The population of Anacostia is predominantly Black. The neighborhood is home to multiple historic and cultural destinations, including the historic home of Frederick Douglass, famous orator and leader of the Abolitionist Movement. In the mid-2000s, Harriet Tregoning, then Washington's director of planning, noting the significant cultural divide defined by the river and eyeing the remaining piers and decking of the old 11th Street Bridge, called for a park on the old superstructure above the river (figure 8.5).

Figure 8.5. 11th Street Bridge park concept. (Credit: Copyright OMA and SAN)

It would be a new public space that would "connect the long-divided neighborhoods."

Aware of the incredible success of the High Line elevated pedestrian park in Manhattan, Scott Kratz, director of the 11th Street Bridge Project, initiated a student design competition, and the project took off. The reimagined bridge space would be more than a park; it would be a major public space and a "destination for neighborhood life," as Jason Long, one of the project architects, put it. There would be trees, art displays, running paths, and places for vendors and food trucks.[20]

Starting out at the Bridge Park, I traced out a loop trying to link parks, historic and cultural sites, commercial enclaves, schools, restaurants, and shops (figure 8.6). For the purposes of this thought experiment, I tried to follow the pleasant, shaded streets with good sidewalks and follow routes with mixed uses. However, in many instances, establishing a town walk will call for upgrading sidewalks where needed with

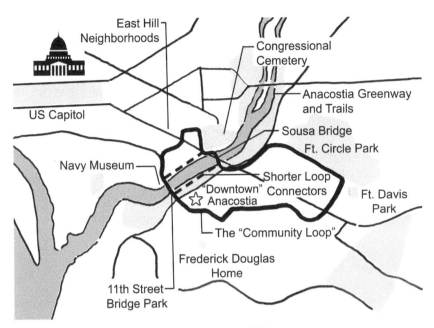

Figure 8.6. Anacostia town walk concept. (Credit: Bill Neumann)

better walking surfaces, more shade, and other improvements. I saw opportunities to link places together, going north into the Sixth Ward, passing the US Naval Museum and the Congressional Cemetery. The loop would then head south, cross the Sousa Bridge where there is access to the Anacostia riverfront parks and trails, then connect to Fort Circle Park. There it would follow the existing Fort Circle Park trail system. Next it would pass near the historic Douglass House and tie back to the 11th Street Park, going through the Anacostia commercial district. I found the area offers all the key ingredients of a great town walk: cultural destinations, parks and greenways, mixed-use areas, shops, places to dine, and other businesses, and it is readily accessible to thousands of residents. There are also Metro stops along the way.

The existing trails along the Anacostia riverbanks could be woven in to form shorter loop options. There is also the potential to form a loop by using the Frederick Douglass Memorial Bridge to the west. Depending on available funds and interest from the community, it could be a deluxe version modeled after the highly developed Denver 5280 Trail or could work as a more rudimentary project following the streets with the better sidewalks and marking the way with simple signage or other markings. And over time it could evolve with more improvements.

When I spoke with Scott Kratz about the loop idea, he stressed the importance of places like the park and the connections to these places.[21] He noted that some people don't even know where the river is, that it has been blocked off by freeways and other big installations.

Conclusion: Engaging Ancient and Future Technologies

Grand loops and town walks are about enabling and being enabled by the ability of humans to walk and stroll. This ability is both efficient and liberating because on foot we can travel on just about any terrain and enjoy doing it on all manner of routes. Increasingly, there are mechanical assistance devices that enable more flexible travel by people with disabilities. On-foot travel is the key liberating factor in the ways we can plan and design this new layer of green infrastructure.

The ideas expressed in this book are, to say the least, ambitious. We're talking about setting out to implement a new template that will reshape cities and change people's behaviors for the better. It's nothing less than adding a new green layer to our urbanized and urbanizing places. It's not an easy task, but it's doable. The good news is that grand loops and town walks already exist in several places. This is enabling too.

It significantly helps that we have the legacy of greenways to build on. They, too, started with an idea, and in less than a generation they have become common green, recreational infrastructure, with neglected rivers and abandoned rail routes transformed into linear parks worldwide. Grand loops and town walks build on this foundation by taking it to a new level. It's a necessary next step because it gives us a geometry that can broadly expand green spaces to make cities more livable and inclusive and bring us health, solace, and fun. And with the increasing crowding of existing outdoor spaces, they will help ensure that the next generation will have places to roam and ramble and experience the outdoors.

As we look at emerging mobility technologies, we see new perspectives and opportunities. One of the most significant changes coming is evolving mobile apps. As phone mobility apps improve and devices become more reliable, we can anticipate far better mapping and positional software. These devices have great potential for people to find and follow desirable grand loop and town walk routes.

Another potential change is the technology of agriculture and how it might affect land uses. With more efficient greenhouse production of vegetables and other produce and the potentials for synthesized meats, we may see over time the obsolescence of traditional farming and ranching. This suggests potentials for more vacant land that could become open space, with increasing consideration of the rural economic benefits of trail recreation.

The key is to craft an inspiring vision, articulate the benefits, and cite the examples. This book is offered as a starting point with concepts and tools to catalyze projects. Now the ball's in your court. As Michael Lydon and Anthony Garcia put it in their book *Tactical Urbanism*, "We are at a fascinating if not daunting moment in time. . . . As rapid urbanization continues one thing is clear. . . . We have to do more with less—*doing* being the operative word."[22]

Notes

Prologue

1. Bernard Ollivier, *The Winds of the Steppe*, translated by Dan Golembeski (New York: Sky Horse Publishing, 2020), 71.

Introduction

1. Thich Nhat Hanh, *How to Walk* (Berkeley: Parallax Press, 2015), 8.

2. M. Trott, R. Driscoll, E. Irlado, and S. Pardhan. "Changes and Correlates of Screen Time in Adults and Children during the COVID-19 Pandemic: A Systematic Review and Meta-Analysis," *eClinicalMedicine* 48 (2022): 101452, doi:10.1016/j.eclinm.2022.101452, https://www.ncbi.nlm.nih.gov/pmc/articles/PMC9122783/.

3. Division of Nutrition, Physical Activity, and Obesity, Centers for Disease Control, "Health Equity Resources," 2022, https://www.cdc.gov/nccdphp/dnpao/health-equity/health-equity-resources.html.

4. Mayo Clinic, "Walking: Trim Your Waistline, Improve Your Health," May 19, 2021, https://www.mayoclinic.org/healthy-lifestyle/fitness/in-depth/walking/art-20046261.

5. Outdoor Industry Association, "Increase in Outdoor Activity Due to COVID 19," August 13, 2020, https://outdoorindustry.org/article/increase-outdoor-activities-due-covid-19/.

6. Centers for Disease Control and Prevention, "Pedestrian Safety," updated

May 2022, https://www.cdc.gov/transportationsafety/pedestrian_safety
/index.html.

7. Centers for Disease Control and Prevention, "More People Walk to Better
Health," updated August 6, 2013, https://www.cdc.gov/vitalsigns/walk
ing/index.html#: ~: text=Walking% 20is% 20the% 20most% 20popular,
minutes% 20in% 20the% 20previous% 20week. &text=Adults% 20who
% 20walk% 20for% 20transportation,6% 20percent% 20in% 205%
20years. https://travelmedium.com/most-popular-outdoor-activities.

8. Jessica Boehm, "I Just Can't Believe We Finished": 315-Mile Trail Loop
around Maricopa County Completed," AZ Central, August 13, 2020.
https://www.azcentral.com/story/news/local/phoenix/2018/11/23/mari
copa-county-finishes-315-mile-trail-around-valley-hiking-biking-regional
-park/2057310002/.

9. "The Jeju Olle Trail," Wikipedia, accessed October 19, 2022, https://
en.wikipedia.org/wiki/Jeju_Olle_Trail.

10. Erin Ryan, "100 Miles of Awesome: Checking In on the Vegas Valley Rim
Trail," *Las Vegas Weekly*, March 22, 2014, https://lasvegasweekly.com/as
-we-see-it/2014/mar/22/100-miles-awesome-checking-vegas-valley-rim
-trail/.

11. Tre Pryor, "Louisville Loop Trail Marches On," *Louisville Homes Blog*,
accessed October 18, 2022, https://louisvillehomesblog.com/news
/louisville-loop-trail-marches-on/.

12. Robert Searns, "The Grand Loop Trail: A Trekking Route through Foothills & Prairie along the Edges of Metro Denver," August 2019, http://
www.metrotrail.org/the-grand-loop-trail.html.

13. Toronto and Region Conservation Authority, "Trail Strategy for the
Greater Toronto Region," September 2019, https://trcaca.s3. ca-central-1.

14. Presidio Museum, "Turquoise Trail," August 13, 2020, accessed October
18, 2022, http://tucsonpresidio.com/turquoise-trail/.

15. Ashville Urban Trail, "Following the Urban Trail, A Walking Tour of the
City's History," accessed October 18, 2022, https://www.exploreasheville
.com/urban-trail/.

16. Jon Murray, "5280 Trail Aims to Be Denver's Answer to New York City's
High Line," *The Denver Post*, August 13, 2020, https://www.denverpost
.com/2019/08/21/denver-5280-trail-urban-loop/.

17. Daniel Hess, Hiroki Hata, and Ernest Sternberg, "Pathways and Artifacts: Neighborhood Design for Physical Activity," *Journal of Urbanism*, 6, no. 1 (2013): 52–71, http://dx.doi.org/10.1080/17549175.2013.765904.

18. Ibid., 56.

19. "21,300 Acres of A.T. Landscape Permanently Protected," press release, the Appalachian Trail Conservancy, March 2022. https://appalachiantrail.org/news/grafton-forest-at-landscape-protected/.

20. See Embercombe website: https://embercombe.org/wp-content/uploads/2022/03/Hemispheres_March_2022_p22.pdf.

21. US Environmental Protection Agency, "Carbon Pollution from Transportation," May 19, 2022, https://www.epa.gov/transportation-air-pollution-and-climate-change/carbon-pollution-transportation#: ~: text=% E2% 80% 8BGreenhouse% 20gas% 20(GHG)% 20emissions, terms% 20 than% 20any% 20other% 20sector.

Chapter 1

1. Robert Macfarlane, *The Old Ways* (New York: Penguin, September 2013), 16.

2. Ben Ryder Howe, "Who Gets to Fish in a Billionaire's Back Yard?" *The New York Times*, September 4, 2022, https://www.nytimes.com/2022/09/01/business/colorado-rivers-fishing-lawsuit.html.

3. Ken Ilgunas, *This Land Is Our Land* (Toronto: Plume, April 2018).

4. Ronda Chapman et al., "Parks and an Equitable Recovery," *Trust for Public Land*, May 2021, https://www.tpl.org/parks-and-an-equitable-recovery-parkscore-report.

5. Michael Booth, "Managing Crowded Parks Raises Equity, Access Concerns," March 20, 2022, https://apnews.com/article/technology-travel-colorado-denver-parks-353fca80777007ff901db0a3ac36791d.

6. Robert M. Searns, "The Evolution of Greenways as an Adaptive Urban Landscape Form," *Landscape and Urban Planning* 33 (1995): 65–80.

7. John Ormsbee Simonds, *Landscape Architecture: A Manual of Planning and Design* (New York: McGraw Hill Professional, 2006): 123–4.

8. "Eastern Parkway, 10 Streets that Changed America," WTTW News, https://interactive.wttw.com/ten/streets/eastern-parkway.

9. Ibid.

10. Ibid.

11. "Eastern Parkway," Wikimedia Foundation, August 28, 2022, https://en.wikipedia.org/wiki/Eastern_Parkway.

12. Thomas Herrera-Mischler, "Olmsted's Buffalo Park System and Its Stewards," Buffalo Toronto Public Media, WNED PBS, 2014, https://www.wned.org/television/wned-productions/wned-history-productions/frederick-law-olmsted-designing-america/learn-more-olmsted/olmsteds-buffalo-park-system/.

13. Robert M. Searns, *Greenways: The Beginning of an International Movement* (Amsterdam: Elsevier, 1996): 60.

14. William H. Whyte, *The Last Landscape* (Philadelphia: University of Pennsylvania Press, 1968): 163.

15. Charles Little, *Greenways for America* (Baltimore: JHU Press, 1990): 23–24.

16. Ibid., 42–43.

17. Ibid., 2.

18. Mike Oppland, "8 Traits of Flow According to Mihaly Csikszentmihalyi," PositivePsychology.com, December 16, 2016, https://positivepsychology.com/mihaly-csikszentmihalyi-father-of-flow/#:~:text=In%20Csikszentmihalyi's%20words%2C%20flow%20is,doing%20it%E2%80%9D%20(1990).

19. Tony Boone, "Outside: Going Downhill on a Bicycle," *Bonedale Amplified. Magazine*, May 2018, https://bonedaleamplified.com/2018/05/magazine/may-2018/outside-still-going-down-hill-on-a-bicycle/.

20. Interview with R. J. Cardin, August 2022.

21. "Origins of the Term 40-Mile-Loop," 40-Mile Loop Land Trust, January 16, 2022, https://40mileloop.org/.

22. Interview with R. J. Cardin, August 30, 2022.

23. "About Us," Vegas Valley Rim Trail, https://vegasvalleyrimtrail.org/home/about-us/.

24. "Vegas Valley Rim Trail," Get Outdoors Nevada, https://vegasvalleyrimtrail.org/.

25. Anna Jean Kaiser, "Hiking a 110-Mile Trail—Entirely within Rio," *OZY*, August 2017, https://www.ozy.com/around-the-world/hiking-a-110-mile-jungle-trail-entirely-within-rio/79063/?

utm_source=pdb&utm_medium=email&utm_campaign=08022017&
variable=86aa1623c19ef3e294ffd13e7a8c80.

26. "Economic Impact Figures Released," Indianapolis Cultural Trail website, July 2015, https://indyculturaltrail.org/2015/07/23/economic-impact -figures-released/#: ~: text=Indianapolis% 20Cultural% 20Trail% 20 has% 20Positive% 20Economic% 20Impact&text=The% 20report% 20 found% 20that% 20property, billion% 20in% 20assessed% 20property% 20value.

27. Jon Murray, "5280 Trail Aims to Be Denver's Answer to New York City's High Line," *Denver Post*, August 2019, https://www.denverpost.com/2019 /08/21/denver-5280-trail-urban-loop/.

28. Kirk Spitzer, "Secrets from the Longest-Living Place on Earth," *AARP Bulletin*, May 2014, https://www.aarp.org/health/healthy-living/info-2014 /longevity-secrets-from-japan.html.

29. "Cities & Neighborhoods," *Walk Score*, 2021, https://www.walkscore .com/cities-and-neighborhoods/.

30. National Complete Streets Coalition, "The Best Complete Streets Policies of 2018," May 2019, https://smartgrowthamerica.org/resources/the-best -complete-streets-policies-of-2018/.

Chapter 2

1. "What Is Ragnar?," Run Ragnar website, 2022, https://www.runragnar .com/ragnar.

2. "The Legacy Trail History," Trail Info/Friends of the Legacy Trail website, https://www.friendsofthelegacytrail.org/the-legacy-trail/.

3. Chelle Grald, "Horses as Trail Users," *American Trails*, July 2018, https:// www.americantrails.org/resources/horses-as-trail-users.

4. Jan Hancock et al., *The Equestrian Guide Handbook* (Washington, D.C.: US Forest Service, 2007).

5. "About Us," Car Free Key West website, 2020, https://www.carfreekey west.com/.

6. Charles Little, *Greenways for America* (Baltimore: Johns Hopkins University Press, 1990).

7. Charles Flink, *The Greenways Imperative* (Gainesville: University Press of Florida, 2020): 281.

8. "Explore the Trail," The Sun Corridor Trail website, 2022, https://suncor ridortrail.org/.

9. "Garden City Movement," Wikipedia, October 16, 2022.

Chapter 3

1. Francis Sanzaro, "The Next Walk You Take Could Change Your Life," *The New York Times*, September 15, 2022, https://www.nytimes.com/2022/09 /15/opinion/walking-mindfulness-benefits.html.

2. Peter Harnik and Jeff Simms, "How Far to Your Nearest Park?," *The Trust for Public Land*, 2004, http://cloud.tpl.org/pubs/ccpe_Distance_from_a _Park.pdf.

3. Mike Lydon and Anthony Garcia, *Tactical Urbanism* (Washington, D.C.: Island Press, 2015).

4. Ryan P. Scott, "Shared Streets, Park Closures and Environmental Justice during a Pandemic Emergency in Denver, Colorado," *Journal of Transport and Health* 21 (June 2021).

5. Johnny Diaz, "Cities Close Streets to Cars, Opening Space for Social Distancing," *The New York Times*, April 11, 2020.

6. "Oakland Slow Streets: Essential Places," About/City of Oakland website, July 2022, https://www.oaklandca.gov/projects/oakland-slow-streets.

7. Kate Darby Rauch, "Berkeley Ends Its 'Healthy Streets' Road Barrier Program," *Berkeleyside*, December 1, 2021, https://www.berkeleyside.org /2021/12/01/healthy-streets-ending.

8. Winnie Hu, "How New York City Lost 63 Miles of Pedestrian-Friendly Open Streets," *The New York Times*, August 11, 2022, https://www.ny times.com/2022/08/11/nyregion/open-streets-nyc.html.

9. "Open Streets Forever," *Transportation Alternatives*, October 2021, https: //www.transalt.org/open-streets-forever-nyc.

10. "Shared Streets Program Development," Denver City website, https:// www.denvergov.org/Government/Agencies-Departments-Offices/Agen cies-Departments-Offices-Directory/Department-of-Transportation-and -Infrastructure/Programs-Services/Shared-Streets.

11. "Atlanta Street Art Map," Street Art Map website, https://streetartmap .org/.

12. Interview with Jeff Olson, September 30, 2021.

13. "Urban and Peri-Urban Forestry," Food and Agriculture Organization of the United Nations, October 2017, https://www.fao.org/forestry/urban forestry/87025/en/#: ~: text=Urban% 20forests% 20can% 20be% 20 defined, and% 20trees% 20in% 20derelict% 20corners.

Chapter 4

1. Amy Camp, *Deciding on Trails* (independently published, December 2020): 160.

2. "Trail Strategy for the Greater Toronto Region: Growing Our Legacy," Toronto and Region Conservation Authority, September 2019, https:// trca.ca/conservation/lands/trail-strategy/.

3. "SF Better Streets—A Guide for Making Street Improvements in San Francisco," City & County of San Francisco, https://www.sfbetterstreets .org/.

4. Edward O'Donnell, Andrew Knab, and Lorene Athey, "Sidewalks and Shared-Use Paths: Safety, Security, and Maintenance," University of Delaware, 2006, https://udspace.udel.edu/handle/19716/3255; "Principles of Pedestrian Planning," *BRT Planning Guide*, https://brtguide.itdp.org /branch/master/guide/pedestrian-access/principles-of-pedestrian-planning.

5. John P. O'Brien and Brad Marston, "A Changing PCT: Climate Change Is Already Altering the Trail Experience," Pacific Crest Trail Organization, March 31, 2022, https://www.pcta.org/2022/a-changing-pct-90289/#: ~: text=In% 20a% 20drier% 20and% 20hotter, the% 20drying% 20of% 20the% 20land.

6. A. M. Koontz, D. Ding, Y. K. Jan, S. de Groot, and A. Hansen, "Wheeled Mobility," *BioMed Research International* (2015): 138176. https://doi.org /10.1155/2015/138176.

7. Bill Norman, "Canes, Crutches, and Walkers," *Quest Magazine*. Muscular Dystrophy Organization, October 2007.

8. "Staunton State Park Track-Chair Program," Colorado Parks and Wildlife webpage, https://cpw.state.co.us/placestogo/parks/Staunton/Pages/Track -Chair-Program.aspx.

Chapter 5

1. Interview with Chuck Flink.

2. Charles Flink, Robert Searns, and Loring Schwarz, *Greenways* (Washington, D.C.: Island Press, 1993): 110.

3. Interview with Elizabeth Stolfus, July 23, 2022.

4. B. A. Wright, R. A. Kaiser, and S. Nicholls, "Rural Landowner Liability for Recreational Injuries: Myths, Perceptions, and Realities," *Journal of Soil and Water Conservation* (May 2002), https://www.jswconline.org /content/57/3/183.

5. "Legal Issues Associated with Trails: An Introduction," Headwaters Economics, Summer 2016, p. 3, https://headwaterseconomics.org/wp -content/uploads/trails-library-legal-overview.pdf.

6. National Association of City Transportation Officials, "Sidewalks," in *Urban Street Design Guide*, (Washington, D.C.: Island Press, 2013), https: //nacto.org/publication/urban-street-design-guide/street-design-elements /sidewalks/.

7. "Handrails: Basis of Design," Great Rivers Greenway/Trail Design Guidelines, https://greatriversgreenway.org/design-guidelines/trail-design/hand rails-basis-design/#: ~: text=Per% 20ADAAG% 2C% 20Handrails% 20 are% 20required, where% 20fall% 20heights% 20exceed% 2030% E2% 80% 9D.

8. AASHTO Task Force on Geometric Design, *AASHTO Guide for the Development of Bicycle Facilities*, (Washington, D.C.: American Association of State Highway and Transportation Officials, 2012).

9. Interview with R. J. Cardin, August 2022.

10. "Maricopa County Regional Trail System Master Plan," Maricopa County Trail Commission, 2004, https://www.maricopacountyparks.net/assets /1/6/MaricopaTrailMasterPlan.pdf.

11. "5280 Trail Draft Design Guidelines," Downtown Denver Partnership and Civitas, 2019, https://www.downtowndenver.com/wp-content /uploads/5280-Draft-Design-Guidelines-8.20.19. pdf.

12. "Complete Streets," Smart Growth America and National Complete Streets Coalition website, https://smartgrowthamerica.org/what-are-com plete-streets/#: ~: text=A% 20complete% 20street% 20may% 20include, lanes% 2C% 20roundabouts% 2C% 20and% 20more.

13. "Pedestrian Lane," Small Town and Rural Design Guide website, https:// ruraldesignguide.com/visually-separated/pedestrian-lane.

14. Ibid. A number of cities have good examples of programs, including St. Charles, Minnesota; Duck, North Carolina; and Detroit, Oregon.

15. "Road Diet Informational Guide," US Department of Transportation Federal Highway Administration, November 2014, https://safety.fhwa.dot.gov/road_diets/guidance/info_guide/ch2.cfm.

16. "Road Design, 11. Roadway Narrowing," US Department of Transportation Federal Highway Administration, https://safety.fhwa.dot.gov/safer journey1/library/countermeasures/11.htm.

17. Global Designing Cities Initiative, "Laneways and Alleys," adapted by *Global Street Design Guide* (Washington, D.C.: Island Press, 2016), https://globaldesigningcities.org/publication/global-street-design-guide/streets/pedestrian-priority-spaces/laneways-and-alleys/.

18. "Laneways We Love," The Laneway Project, https://www.thelanewayproject.ca/lanewayswelove.

19. *The Manual on Uniform Traffic Control Devices*, published by the Federal Highway Administration, provides the sign specifications. https://mutcd.fhwa.dot.gov/.

20. Available on the Minnesota Department of Natural Resources webpage, https://www.dnr.state.mn.us/publications/trails_waterways/index.html.

21. National Association of City Transportation Officials, *Urban Street Design Guide* (Washington, D.C.: Island Press, 2013).

22. *The Manual on Uniform Traffic Control Devices*, published by the Federal Highway Administration, provides the standards. https://mutcd.fhwa.dot.gov/.

23. Mike Lydon and Anthony Garcia, *Tactical Urbanism* (Washington, D.C.: Island Press, 2015).

24. Neil Porter Brown, "Making Art Work," *Harvard Magazine*, September/October 2022, p. 51, https://www.harvardmagazine.com/2022/09/alumni-david-andersson.

Chapter 6

1. Ben Mauk, "Building the First Long-Distance Hiking Trail in Kurdistan," *The New York Times*, April 20, 2022, https://www.nytimes.com/2022/04/20/magazine/hiking-kurdistan.html.

2. "Regional Open Space Plan," Southern Nevada Regional Planning Coalition, adopted July 2006, p. 2.

3. Jon Murray, "5280 Trail Aims to Be Denver's Answer to New York City's

High Line," *The Denver Post*, August 21, 2019, https://www.denverpost
.com/2019/08/21/denver-5280-trail-urban-loop/.

4. Charles Flink, *The Greenway Imperative* (Gainesville: University of Florida
Press, March 2020).

5. "Reports and Charts," LandVote webpage, Trust for Public Land, 2020,
https://tpl.quickbase.com/db/bbqna2qct? a=dbpage&pageID=8.

6. "Stapleton Development Plan," Forest City Development, March 1995,
pp. 5–22, https://www.denvergov.org/content/dam/denvergov/Portals
/646/documents/planning/Plans/Stapleton_Development_Plan.pdf.

7. Ibid, 10 and 11.

8. Flink, *The Greenway Imperative*, 178–215.

9. See the "5280 Trail" page on the Downtown Denver Partnership website,
https://www.downtowndenver.com/initiatives-and-planning/the-5280/.

10. See the "Wolf River Greenway" page on the Wolf River Conservancy
website, https://wolfriver.org/the-wolf-river-greenway.

11. Arch Aerial provides aerial mapping services, https://archaerial.com
/aerial-mapping/.

12. Gary Richards, "Fixing 'Worst Interchange in Region' Could Cost $1
Billion: Roadshow," *The Mercury News*, December 2020, https://www
.mercurynews.com/2020/12/12/gulp-fixing-101-880-mess-could-cost-1
-billion-roadshow/.

13. See the American Trails resources webpage, https://www.americantrails
.org/resources/construction-and-maintenance-costs-for-trails.

14. "New Research Finds Public Investment in Trails, Walking and Biking
Infrastructure Delivers Potential Economic Benefits of $138.5 Billion
Annually," Rails to Trails Conservancy, October 2019, https://www
.railstotrails.org/resource-library/resources/new-research-finds-public-in
vestment-in-trails-walking-and-biking-infrastructure-delivers-potential
-economic-benefits-of-1385-billion-annually/.

15. Courtney S. Suess, "Measuring the Economic Impact of the Vegas Valley
Rim Trail." Prepared for the Outside Las Vegas Foundation, University of
Nevada Las Vegas, 2013, p. 12.

16. "Economic Impact Figures Released," The Indianapolis Cultural Trail,
July 2015, https://indyculturaltrail.org/2015/07/23/economic-impact
-figures-released/#: ~: text=Indianapolis% 20Cultural% 20Trail% 20has

% 20Positive% 20Economic% 20Impact&text=The% 20report% 20
found% 20that% 20property, billion% 20in% 20assessed% 20property%
20value.

Chapter 7

1. Interview with R. J. Cardin, August 2022.

2. Charles Flink, *The Greenway Imperative* (Gainesville: University Press of
Florida, 2020): 10–20.

3. "Sports and Exercise among Americans," *TED: The Economics Daily,* US
Bureau of Labor Statistics, August 2016, https://www.bls.gov/opub/ted
/2016/sports-and-exercise-among-americans.htm#: ~: text=Walking%
20was% 20the% 20most% 20popular, average% 20day% 20engaged%
20in% 20walking.

4. "Outdoor Foundation Study: Half of the US Population Did Not Participate in Outdoor Recreation in 2019," The Outdoor Industry Association,
December 2020, https://outdoorindustry.org/resource/2020-outdoor
-participation-report/.

5. Paige Waehner, "Motivation for Exercise," *Verywell Fit,* October 2021,
https://www.verywellfit.com/fitness-motivation-4157145.

6. Pedro J. Teixeira et al., "Exercise Motivation, Eating, and Body Image
Variables as Predictors of Weight Control," *Medicine and Science in Sports
and Exercise* 38(1) (January 2006): 179–88, doi:10.1249/01.mss.0000
180906.10445.8d.

7. Amanda O'Donnell, "Why the Group 'Hot Girl Walks' Popping Up
around Texas Are Kind of Beautiful," *Texas Monthly,* September 2022,
https://www.texasmonthly.com/travel/texas-hot-girl-walk-austin-dallas
-katy-trail-tik-tok/.

8. Daniel Baldwin Hess et al., "Pathways and Artifacts: Neighborhood
Design for Physical Activity," *Journal of Urbanism* 6(1) (2013): 52–71,
http://dx.doi.org/10.1080/17549175.2013.765904.

9. Ibid., 2.

10. Ibid., 52.

11. Ibid., 57.

12. Ibid., 57–58.

13. Ibid., 58–59.

14. Ibid., 64.

15. Brett Durett, "Causes of Backpacking and Hiking Deaths," *Brett's Random Musings* blog post, May 2016, https://brett.durrett.net/causes-of-back packing-and-hiking-deaths/.

16. "Odds of Dying," Injury Facts, National Safety Council, 2022, https://injuryfacts.nsc.org/all-injuries/preventable-death-overview/odds-of -dying/.

17. Giffords Law Center Statistics webpage, https://giffords.org/lawcenter /gun-violence-statistics/.

18. Angie Schmitt, *Right of Way* (Washington, D.C.: Island Press, 2020).

19. Kea Wilson, "Fear of Assault Keeps Women from Walking," *Streetsblog*, June 2021, https://usa.streetsblog.org/2021/06/28/fear-of-assault-keeps -women-from-walking/.

20. "Rail-Trails and Safe Communities: The Experience on 372 Trails," Rails-to-Trails Conservancy, 1998, p. 14, https://safety.fhwa.dot.gov/ped_bike /docs/rt_safecomm.pdf.

21. Amanda Machado, "Why People of Color Often Feel Unsafe in the Outdoors," *Sierra*, 2020, https://www.sierraclub.org/sierra/why-people-color -often-feel-unsafe-outdoors.

22. See the Blackpackers website, https://blackpackers.org/.

23. Interview with Charles Brown, April 6, 2022.

24. "1 in 4 US Adults Live with a Disability," Centers for Disease Control and Prevention, August 2018, https://www.cdc.gov/media/releases/2018 /p0816-disability.html.

25. "The Aging Readiness & Competitiveness Report 2021," *AARP Bulletin* (2021): 38. https://www.aarpinternational.org/file% 20library/arc/aarp -arc-3.0-report.pdf.

26. Webpage for the 4T, https://www.4t-trail.org/.

27. Gregory Scruggs, "The Cities Trailblazing Transit Service into the Wilderness," *Next City*, June 2021, https://nextcity.org/urbanist-news/the-cities -trailblazing-transit-service-into-the-wilderness.

28. Representative Jimmy Gomez, "Congressman Gomez and Senator Booker Introduce Transit to Trails Act of 2012," press release, April 2021, https://gomez.house.gov/news/documentsingle.aspx? DocumentID=2388.

29. Lopez, Meghan Lopez, "Jefferson County Open Space Partners with Lyft to Try to Reduce Trail Congestion," *Denver 7*, July 2021, https://www .denver7. com/news/local-news/jefferson-county-open-space-partners -with-lyft-to-try-to-reduce-trail-congestion.

30. Jamie Siebrase, "Easy Hikes You Can Absolutely Do with Your Kids," *ColoradoParent*, Summer 2021, https://www.coloradoparent.com /family-friendly-hikes-denver/.

31. "What Is Included in Wellness Programs? A Checklist for Employers," *Go365*, March 2022, https://www.go365. com/articles/what-is-included -in-wellness-programs.

32. "Little Rock's Innovative Medical Mile," Case Study, City Parks Alliance, 2022, https://cityparksalliance.org/resource/medical-mile-little-rock/.

33. "School Programs," Wolf River Conservancy website, https://wolfriver .org/school-programs.

34. "SPREE Summer Camp," The Greenway Foundation website, https:// thegreenwayfoundation.org/spree/camps/summer/.

35. "About Our Program," Sierra Club website, https://www.sierraclub.org /ico/about-our-program.

36. "US Ecommerce Forecast 2022 Report Preview," EMarketer and Insider Intelligence website, https://www.insiderintelligence.com/resources /us-ecommerce-forecast-2022/? itm_source=homepage.

37. See travelingjules.com.

38. World Tourism Organization, "Walking Tourism—Promoting Regional Development, Executive Summary," UNWTO, Madrid, https://doi.org /10.18111/9789284420520.

39. Interview with Jan Hancock, August 31, 2022.

Chapter 8

1. James Brasuell, "An Aggressive Plan to Build Out Dallas Trail System Is a Winner," *Dallas Morning News*, June 10, 2014, https://www.dallasnews .com/opinion/editorials/20140608-editorial-aggressive-plan-to-build-out -dallas-trail-system-is-a-winner.ece.

2. Stephanie Lamm, "Feeing Crowded Yet Dallas/Fort Worth Gained 1 Million People in Less Than a Decade," *Dallas Morning News*, April 19,

2029, https://www.dallasnews.com/business/2019/04/19/feeling-crowded
-yet-dallas-fort-worth-gained-1-million-people-in-less-than-a-decade/.

3. North Central Texas Council of Governments, Veloweb Map, accessed
October 23, 2022, https://www.nctcog.org/nctcg/media/Transportation
/DocsMaps/Plan/Bike/Veloweb.pdf.

4. Cameron Dodd, "Lone Star Walkabout: A Hiker Sets Off to Be the First
to Walk the 130-Mile Northeast Texas Trail," *Texas Parks and Wildlife
Monthly*, November 2013, https://tpwmagazine.com/archive/2013/nov
/ed_1_trail/index.phtml.

5. Macrotrends, "Toronto Canada Population 1950–2022," accessed October 23, 2022, https://www.macrotrends.net/cities/20402/toronto/popula
tion#: ~: text=The% 20current% 20metro% 20area% 20population, a%
200.94% 25% 20increase% 20from% 202019.

6. "What You Need to Know about Ontario's Plan to Grow the Size of the
Greenbelt," JD Supra, June 19, 2021, https://www.jdsupra.com
/legalnews/what-you-need-to-know-ontario-s-plan-to-8870554/.

7. The Bruce Trail Conservancy, accessed October 23, 2023, https://bruce
trail.org/.

8. Trans Canada Trail, "Welcome to the Trans Canada Trail," accessed October 23, 2022, https://tctrail.ca/.

9. Toronto and Region Conservation Authority, "Trail Strategy for the
Greater Toronto Region," September 2019, https://trcaca.s3. ca-central-1
. amazonaws.com/app/uploads/2019/09/30102454/TRCA_TrailStrategy
-2019-Sept-update-FA-sglpgs.pdf.

10. "Buffalo–Niagara Falls Metropolitan Area," Wikipedia, accessed October
23, 2022, https://en.wikipedia.org/wiki/Buffalo% E2% 80% 93Niagara
_Falls_metropolitan_area.

11. David Russell Schilling, "Buffalo: The Best Designed & Planned City in
the United States," *Industry Tap*, January 25, 2015, https://www.industry
tap.com/buffalo-best-designed-planned-city-united-states/26019.

12. Niagara Falls Canada, *The Niagara Parkway*, June 29, 2018, https://www
.niagarafallstourism.com/blog/the-niagara-parkway/.

13. Erie Country Environment and Planning, "Shoreline Trail," accessed
October 23, 2022, https://www2. erie.gov/environment/index.php? q=
shoreline-trail.

14. Thomas J. Prohaska, "Plan Would Extend Greenway Trail along Lake Ontario," *The Buffalo News*, accessed February 18, 2022, https://buffalo news.com/news/local/plan-would-extend-greenway-trail-along-lake -ontario-shore/article_df66b1f4–7844–11eb-9f21–0710a25a1607. html.

15. Kyle Munzenrieder, "Florida Now Officially the Third Most Populous State," *Miami New Times*, December, 23, 2014, https://www.miaminew times.com/news/florida-is-now-officially-the-third-most-populous-state -6554486.

16. "Total County Population: April 1, 1970–2030," Web10. xls, Florida Demographic Estimating Conference, August 2010, http://edr.state.fl.us /Content/population-demographics/data/Pop_0401_c.pdf.

17. Trust for Public Lands, "Florida Gulf Coast Trail," accessed October 24, 2022, https://www.tpl.org/our-work/florida-gulf-coast-trail.

18. "The Legacy Trail," Sarasota Legacy Trail.com, accessed October 23, 2022, http://www.sarasotalegacytrail.com.

19. Luz Lazo, "D.C.'s First Elevated Park Will Link Neighborhoods Divided by the River," *Washington Post*, August 4, 2022, https://www.washington post.com/transportation/2022/08/04/dc-anacostia-river-park-bridge/.

20. Megan Kimble, "Can Anacostia Build a Bridge without Displacing Its People?," *New York Times*, August 9, 2022, https://www.nytimes.com /interactive/2022/08/09/headway/anacostia-bridge.html See also Laurie Mazur, "Can a Park Prevent Gentrification?," *Next City*, February 10, 2021, https://nextcity.org/urbanist-news/can-a-park-prevent-gentrification.

21. Author interview with Scott Kratz, director, 11th Street Bridge Park, August 19, 2022.

22. Mike Lydon and Anthony Garcia, *Tactical Urbanism* (Washington, D.C.: Island Press, 2015), 210.

Helpful Resources

Following is a list of selected manuals, plans, reports, inspiring books, and knowledgeable organizations. A comprehensive list would be prohibitively long, but many of the publications and websites are outstanding because they are comprehensive. They answer questions and provide handy guidance to anyone contemplating a grand loop or town walk. See also the Notes for additional references and source material.

Planning, Design, and Development

Trail Planning and Development Guidelines: Shared Use, Paved Trails, Natural Surface Trails (St. Paul, Minn.: Department of Natural Resources. Trails and Waterways Division, 2006).

Hugh Duffy, *Trail Assessment, Planning and Design Sketchbook*, 2007 Edition, https://www.americantrails.org/resources/guide-to-sustainable-mountain -trails.

Maricopa County Regional Trails System Plan, Maricopa County Trail Commission, 2004, https://www.maricopacountyparks.net/assets/1/6/Maricopa TrailMasterPlan.pdf.

Trail Strategy for the Greater Toronto Region, https://trcaca.s3.ca-central-1 .amazonaws.com/app/uploads/2019/09/30102454/TRCA_TrailStrategy -2019-Sept-update-FA-sglpgs.pdf.

The Denver 5280 Trail Vision Plan and *Design Guidelines*, https://www.down towndenver.com/wp-content/uploads/5280-Vision-Plan-8.20.19.pdf and

https://www.downtowndenver.com/wp-content/uploads/5280-Draft
-Design-Guidelines-8.20.19.pdf 2019.

Dan Burden et al., *Street Design for Healthy Neighborhoods*, 2002, https://
www.legacy.civicwell.org/wp-content/uploads/2013/08/street-design
-guidelines-for-healthy-neighborhoods-2002.pdf.

Urban Street Design Guide, National Association of City Transportation Officials, 2013, https://nacto.org/publication/urban-street-design-guide/

Walkways Sidewalks and Public Spaces, US Federal Highway Administration,
2022, https://safety.fhwa.dot.gov/ped_bike/univcourse/pdf/swless13.pdf.

Planning and Designing for Pedestrians, San Diego Regional Planning Agency,
2002, https://www.sandag.org/uploads/publicationid/publicationid_713
_3269.pdf.

A Guide to Making Better Street Improvements in San Francisco, City and
County of San Francisco/Better Streets.org, 2015, https://www.sfbetter
streets.org/design-guidelines/street-types/neighborhood-residential-streets/
and https://www.sfbetterstreets.org/design-guidelines/sidewalk-width/.

Institute for Transportation and Development Policy, *The Online BRT Planning Guide*, Chapter 29.1, "Principles of Pedestrian Planning, https://
brtguide.itdp.org/branch/master/guide/pedestrian-access/principles-of
-pedestrian-planning.

Chuck Flink, Kristine Olka, and Robert Searns, *Trails of the 21st Century*
(Washington, D.C.: Island Press, 2001).

Trail Solutions (Boulder, Colo.: International Mountain Biking Association,
2004).

Edward O'Donnell, Andrew Knab, and Lorene Athey, *Sidewalks and Shared-
Use Paths: Safety, Security, and Maintenance* (Newark: Institute for Public
Administration University of Delaware, 2007).

Jan Hancock et al., *Equestrian Design Guidebook for Trail, Trailheads and
Campgrounds* (Missoula, Mt.: USDA Forest Service, 2007).

Trails Accessibility Assessment, 2002, https://www.beneficialdesigns.com
/assessment/trails/.

Sidewalk Accessibility Assessment, 2022, https://www.beneficialdesigns.com
/assessment/sidewalks/.

Colorado's Guide to Planning Trails with Wildlife in Mind, 2001, https://cpw
.state.co.us/Documents/Trails/Planning_Trails_with_Wildlife_in_Mind
_full_plan.pdf.

The Louisville Loop Master Plan, Louisville-Jefferson County Metro Government, 2013, https://viewer.joomag.com/louisville-loop-master-plan-loop masterplan-draft-041813sm-0/0714727001517858949.

Robert Searns, *Concept Plan for a Grant Loop Trail*, The Colorado Parks Foundation, 2018, https://metrotrail.org/grand-loop-plan.html.

Organizations

Advice on design, construction, management, fundraising, selling points, case studies, and many other answers.

American Trails: https://www.americantrails.org/

Rails-to-Trails Conservancy: https://www.railstotrails.org/

World Trails Network: https://worldtrailsnetwork.org/

National Association of City Transportation Officials (NACTO): https://nacto.org/publication/urban-street-design-guide/

Smart Growth America (National Complete Streets Coalition): https://smartgrowthamerica.org/what-are-complete-streets/

Pedestrian and Bicycle Information Center (PBIC): https://www.pedbikeinfo.org/

Equitable Cities ("Urban Planning and Policy Research . . . at the intersection of transportation, health and equity"): https://equitablecities.com/

Pennsylvania Land Trust Alliance and Conserve PA: https://landtrustalliance.org https://weconservepa.org/trails/

Guidance

Mark Fenton, *The Complete Guide to Walking* (Guilford, CT: Globe Pequot Press, 2001).

Chuck Flink, *The Greenway Imperative* (Gainesville: University Press of Florida, 2020).

Jeff Olson, *The Third Mode: Towards a Green Society*, TheThirdMode.Com, 2020.

Mike Lydon and Anthony Garcia, *Tactical Urbanism* (Washington, D.C.: Island Press, 2015).

Amy Camp, *Deciding on Trails 7 Practices of Health Trail Towns*, Plug and Play Publishing.com, 2020.

Jeff Speck, *Walkable City* (Grand Rapids, Mich.: Northpoint Press, 2012).

Ray Jardine, *Beyond Back Packing* (Danville, N.H.: AdventureLore Press, 2000).

Charles E. Little, *Greenways for America* (Baltimore, Md.: John Hopkins University Press, 1990).

John Ormsbee Simonds, *Landscape Architecture* (New York: McGraw-Hill, 1961).

Jamie Siebrase, *Mythbusting the Great Outdoors* (Helena, Mt.: Falcon, 2022).

Jamie Siebrase, *Hiking with Kids* (Helena, Mt.: Falcon, 2021).

Inspiration and Ideas

Thich Nhat Hanh, *How To Walk* (Berkeley, Calif.: Parallax Press, 2015.

Annabel Streets, *52 Ways to Walk* (New York: Putnam, 2022).

Robert Macfarlane, *The Old Ways* (London: Penguin Books, 2012).

Robert Moor, *On Trails* (New York: Simon & Schuster, 2016).

Philip Ferranti, *Hiking!* (Seattle, Wash.: Kendall/Hunt Publishing, 1997).

Bernard Ollivier, *Out of Istanbul/Winds of the Steppe/Walking to Samarkand* Trilogy (New York: Skyhorse Publishing, 2019–2020).

Jane Jacobs, *The Death and Life of Great American Cities* (New York: Vintage Books, 1992).

About the Author

Photo by Dru Carroll

Robert Searns has a four-decade trail and greenway history of visualizing concepts, writing effective plans, and getting projects built. He was project director of Denver's Platte River and Mary Carter Greenways, both national-award-winning projects. He coauthored *Greenways: A Guide to Planning, Design, and Development*, contributed to *Greenways: The Beginning of an International Movement*, and has written for *Planning, Landscape Architecture, LA China*, and *American Trails* magazines. Bob also served as editor-in-chief of *Trails and Beyond* magazine, chaired American Trails, and was a founder of the World Trails Network. Bob is a trail enthusiast, walking, hiking, and biking whenever he can.